OLD TIMES IN
THE ADIRONDACKS

The Narrative of a Trip into the Wilderness in 1873

by

SENECA RAY STODDARD

Edited and with Biographical Sketch by

MAITLAND C. DE SORMO

Saranac Lake, New York 12983

ISBN 978-1-4930-7679-6

Printed in the United States of America
By the George Little Press Inc., Burlington, Vermont

Library of Congress Catalog Card Number: 77-182699

Dedication

To the Stoddards—Birdie, Hiram and Ernestine—with sincere appreciation for the kindness, patience and cooperation which made possible my obtaining the incomparable S.R. Stoddard collection.

Table of Contents

List of Illustrations

SENECA RAY STODDARD

Very likely very few New York staters know that the nation's three greatest 19th century photographers were all born here and that their birth-places were less than a hundred miles apart. Mathew B. Brady (1823?-1896) near Lake George in Warren County; William H. Jackson (1843-1942) in Peru, Clinton County, and Seneca Ray Stoddard (1844-1917) in Wilton, Saratoga County.

Brady himself and his staff of talented assistants, as is well known, gained their fame by taking more than 3500 superb Civil War battle pictures and camp scenes. Jackson's fame was soundly based on his memorable photographs and paintings of the West.

S. R. Stoddard, the third of the trio, was unquestionably the most versatile of the group. He was also a talented artist with ink, oils and watercolors; an inventor; a sensitive poet; a chatty, witty writer and one of the most widely-traveled men of his time. Furthermore, he was also a successful editor and magazine publisher.

Two generations ago his name was recognized by discerning people throughout the East as being synonymous with superb outdoor photography. Testimonials from nearly every reputable writer, traveler and authority on the Adirondacks proclaimed in print that his guidebooks and maps were the most popular and reliable such sources available. Newspaper clippings attest that audiences in cities and towns all over the country who heard his eloquent lectures, illustrated by his unique and carefully tinted stereopticon slides, acclaimed such programs as being the most entertaining, natural and educational evenings of that or many other seasons.

In spite of this versatility and seemingly widespread recognition, however, the gifted man from Glens Falls was never accorded the full fame and fortune which he deserved. This apparently paradoxical situation was mainly attributable to his gentle, easy-going, unassuming nature. Unlike his more aggressive, publicity-minded contemporaries—W. H. H. Murray, Verplanck Colvin and Harry V. Radford—Stoddard never sought success as ardently, obsessedly or as persistently as they did. Therefore, his importance was somewhat overlooked or undervalued by the historians of his time.

Ironically enough, the only person who eulogized him at any length confused him with his celebrated distant cousin, John L. Stoddard of Boston, whose published lectures found their way into more than two million homes. The fact is that even today many local libraries and historical societies have surprisingly little Stoddard material on their shelves or in their archives.

Of course the older generation of campers on Lake George and other alluring Adirondack lakes have always valued highly their Stoddard photos and albums, their various editions of his guidebooks and maps. Even more noteworthy have been the desire and enthusiasm shown by the more recent devotees of our incomparable mountain region in their efforts to satisfy their considerable curiosity about the fascinating lore of the places which often lure them back for many unforgettable seasons.

Nowadays Stoddard's incomparable photographic reminders of Lakes George, Champlain, Luzerne, Saratoga, Schroon and such far-famed, long-gone hotels as the Bolton, Crosbyside, Horicon, Katskill

House, Old Fort George and Ft. William Henry; Pearl Point, the Phoenix, the Roger's Rock and the Sagamore; The Wayside at Luzerne; the Leland and the Taylor House at Schroon, the Halfway House—such names and those of many other resorts equally well remembered still evoke reminiscent smiles and evergreen recollections.

Stoddard's camera also recorded for posterity the long-since vanished hotels of the picturesque Placid-Saranac region—the Allen House, the Grand View, the Ruisseaumont (all at Placid); the Riverside, the Berkeley, the Algonquin, the Ampersand, Miller's, the Prospect House (later Saranac Inn), Bartlett's, Corey's Rustic Lodge (Upper Saranac Lake), Paul Smith's, the Loon Lake House; Rainbow Lake House; Ralph's and the Chasm House in the Chateaugay Lakes area.

In the Keene Valley section were the Tahawus House, Beede's, the Willey House (also known as Hurricane Lodge), Adirondack House and the Mount Porter; the Mansion House at Elizabethtown; Moody's and the Tupper Lake House at Tupper; the Prospect and Blue Mountain Houses on Blue Mountain Lake; Hathorn's at Golden Beach, the Antlers, Under the Hemlocks, the Raquette Lake House—all these and many others can now be seen only as pictures—and Stoddard's were invariably the best ever taken. The features of such famous guides as Alvah Dunning, Paul Smith, Bill Nye, Mitchell Sabattis and Old Mountain Phelps were perpetuated in oft-reprinted pictures by Stoddard. Incidentally, the patriarch of Keene Valley, Orson (Old Mountain) Phelps depended on the sale of Stoddard's likenesses of him for a considerable part of his livelihood in his declining years.

Besides being superlative scenes the photographs also represent visible history. The steamboats and guideboats on the lakes and rivers, the ruins of the old forts, the crowded stagecoaches, the ubiquitous toll gates, the survey parties, the lumbermen; the clothing worn, the architecture and furnishings of the luxurious camps and posh hotels—even the musical instruments and the sporting equipment all attract varying degrees of interest from the amateur as well as the professional historians and anthropologists. Seen in such perspective the photographs constitute a priceless heritage, a graphic key to the serenity of yesteryear.

In the opinion of many collectors and camera enthusiasts, the numerous night scenes taken by Stoddard are of special attraction. Most of these were taken by the intense light generated by magnesium powder, a technique that required considerable skill and practice and which occasionally resulted in injury, disfigurement or worse. One such experience, while he was making a night study of the Washington Memorial Arch at the lower end of New York's Fifth Avenue, was nearly fatal for Stoddard.

He described the near miss in a written interview requested by the photography editor of the New York *Tribune* printed on March 2, 1890. Wrote Stoddard: "Instead of boiling up out of the cup, as any well-mannered charge ought to have done, the unusually large amount of magnesium needed to illuminate so large an object, misbehaved. Other guncotton and gunpowder charges have always acted properly, but the force of this one seemed to be downward like dynamite. It exploded with a loud detonation, tore the cup into fragments and boiled down over my head and shoulders in a sheet of flames which singed hair and beard and which seared my hands and the side of my face like a hot iron. So, after I got my slide in and saved my plate, I held an impromptu reception with the policemen and a sympathizing crowd. This was followed by a free ride in an ambulance to St. Vincent's Hospital. But the photograph was entirely successful!"

Another remarkable night view, now considered a classic, was that of the Statue of Liberty. Its sculptor, Bartholdi, later declared that this was the only photograph which ever did it justice. Other examples of his after-dark artistry included scenes of Gibraltar, the Alhambra, the Sphinx, Constantinople's Golden Horn, the Acropolis, St. Paul's in Rome, the Arc de Triomphe and the Paris Exposition of 1900, the Midnight Sun, and Chicago's Columbian Exposition of 1892-3.

Among his more familiar nocturnal Adirondack and American masterpieces were the firelight scenes of the open camps at the Sagamore on Long Lake, the Antlers at Raquette Lake, Camp Phelps on Upper Ausable Lake; the perennially popular poker-playing guides scene, the party of hunters and their dangling deer, and the Colvin survey party at Long Lake in 1888. His night studies taken in Indian huts in Alaska and British Columbia, the Yellowstone and the Yosemite by moonlight are also in a class by themselves for composition and effect.

Very little is known about Seneca Ray Stoddard's early life. He was born on May 13, 1844 in the Saratoga County hamlet of Wilton. His parents were Charles and Hattie (Ray) Stoddard. The family lived on farms in several sections of this state before the father moved to Hartford, Michigan where, at the age of 50, he was killed by a falling tree.

Seneca Ray, like most of the young people of his time, took advantage of the sporadic and now considered inadequate educational opportunities provided for rural children, but he was largely self-taught. In spite of these handicaps he became a very learned man whose wide interests were whetted

11

and satisfied by intensive study and extensive travel.

Leaving home at the age of 16 he worked for the next four years, at the starting pay of $3.00 per week, painting numbers on freight cars and decorative scenes on the interior of passenger coaches. At twenty he moved to Glens Falls and its more photogenic possibilities. His first pictures were small views and stereopticon scenes of the Hudson and the town.

After exhausting the picture-taking potential of the Glens Falls region, he journeyed farther afield on foot, bicycle, stagecoach and train to Lake George, Luzerne, Ticonderoga, Crown Point and Lake Champlain. In the early 1860's he took his first pictures of Ausable Chasm and its geologic wonders.

Besides augmenting his stock of photographs Stoddard started his guidebook series at that time: his first were of Saratoga Springs; then, from 1873-1877, he published annual revisions of his *Lake George-Luzerne-Schroon Lake* and *The Adirondacks*. From 1878-1888 the title was changed to *Lake George* and *Lake Champlain*.

The sequence called *The Adirondacks Illustrated* came out in 1873, following Stoddard's first trip through the mountain region with Charles Oblenis, his brother-in-law (The Professor of the stories), as his companion. The cleverly-written narrative of this journey added much humor and interest to the series, which appeared in appreciable yearly revisions until 1914, three years before Stoddard's death.

The incredibly industrious photographer-guidebook writer also became a competent civil engineer under the tutelage of his half-uncle, Hiram Philo, a well-known Glens Falls surveyor. During the same period, while he was writing his two sets of guidebooks, he was also busy making maps, first of Lake George, then of Lake Champlain and, still later, of the Adirondack area. These, prepared from government surveys and personal notes, and revised often, became the most detailed and authoritative charts to be had.

Undoubtedly the most useful map ever done by Stoddard was his Lake George hydrographic survey of 1906-08. This, reprinted in 1951, became almost indispensable for boat-owners and fishermen on that scenically endowed body of water.

The first of several long trips away from his home base came in 1883. Having become a good canoeist by constant practice on Lake George, Stoddard and Charles Burchard, secretary of the New York chapter of the American Canoe Association, started on the first leg of what became a five-stage cruise from the mouth of the Hudson River along the New England coast to the head of the Bay of Fundy. This exciting expedition, which had been originally planned so that the "Atlantis" was to be used only on sidetrips, became a real ordeal punctuated and almost permanently terminated when they capsized in a gale off Portsmouth, New Hampshire and a seemingly endless hour and a half later, were rescued by fishermen. All this came about because Stoddard and Burchard felt that it would be somewhat cowardly to correct the false impression which the reporters had already created in the New York newspapers. By a rare combination of good luck, good seamanship and—most important—the Good Lord above, the nearly 2,100 mile odyssey was completed during five August vacations and with three different companions.

In 1892 Stoddard went to Alaska with Burchard again as his companion. Although a huge camera of his own invention, designed to take a 20″ X 49½″ curved plate exposure, failed him completely, his trusty smaller Kodak added many more splendid slides to his ever-increasing collection which later became his lecture illustrations.

Early in 1894 he traveled south to Florida, the Gulf

States and Cuba; later that year he went across the continent and photographed the Bad Lands of Dakota, the Yellowstone Park, the cliff dwellings and the Grand Canyon in the Southwest, California's Yosemite Valley and the Pacific Northwest.

In 1895 on the cruise ship "Friesland" he sailed to Bermuda, the Mediterranean countries, the Holy Land, then went north from Italy through Switzerland, France and home again from a British port.

In 1897 on board the "Ohio" he went to England, the Orkney, Faroe and Shetland Islands, Iceland, the North Cape, Denmark, Russia and Germany. Accounts of this and the preceding trip were published in handsome, profusely-illustrated volumes entitled *The Cruise of the Friesland* and *The Midnight Sun*. The expenses of both trips were providently provided for by his selling copies of the book to his fellow passengers, whose pictures also appeared in each volume.

His final European voyage was made in 1900 when, besides photographing the Paris Exposition, he toured Holland, Belgium, England, Scotland and Ireland.

Each of these long journeys resulted in highly-regarded illustrated lectures. Although greatly impressed by Europe, Stoddard still considered American scenery to be the best and the most varied in the world. Furthermore, as he often stated, the most satisfying vistas of them all were those to be found in his own Adirondack region.

His favorite and most popular lecture was called "The Hudson, from the Mountains to the Sea." Typical of audience reaction to this program was the account printed in the *Mail and Express* (New York) following a Chickering Hall appearance on April 25, 1893.

Quote: "Seldom has a more delighted audience

turned away from Chickering Hall than that which reluctantly dispersed after the lecture of S. R. Stoddard last night. Probably never before have such pictures been thrown upon a screen than those 250 marvelous delineations of Adirondack scenery and life. Nor ever were scenes more delightfully described than in his lecture, which corruscated with eloquence, poetry and wit.

"Mr. Stoddard took his audience through the wonderful Adirondack country by a half-dozen different approaches, identifying as he passed, the mountains, the lakes, the streams, the hotels along the way. He took them into the forest's depths, across carries, into club preserves, up mountains and down rapids. He hunted with them, fished with them, introduced them to camp life, lumber and mining camps, to the noted guides—Paul Smith, Old Mountain Phelps, Alvah Dunning and Mitchell Sabattis—and to John Brown of Ossawatamie, now buried at North Elba. Lake George, Lake Champlain and the lonely lakes of the north gave up their loveliest views at the beck of the lecturer's wand.

"To gather material for this great work Mr. Stoddard has gone over all the ground personally, penetrating the depths of the wilderness by obscure trails, living in rough camps and often on short rations, enduring great fatigue and sparing no care or expense to get the desired results. Results which in many cases have furnished piratical competitors with their main stock in trade.

"Through his maps, his guidebooks, his photographs and more recently his lectures, Mr. Stoddard has done more than any other man to popularize this marvelous region and to make its beauties and advantages known. Frequent applause interrupted the lecturer and at the close many stopped to congratulate him on his success. It ought not to be his last appearance before a New York City audience."

Unquestionably the most effective and most timely lecture on the Adirondacks was that given on February 26, 1892 in the Assembly Chamber of the State Legislature in Albany. Under the auspices of the Forest Commission Stoddard had been invited to show the legislators and their guests the condition of things "up in the woods." The real purpose of the meeting was to obtain favorable action on pending legislation which would create the Adirondack Park.

A reporter for the *Argus* described the program as follows: "No similar event ever given in Albany has attracted the very general interest displayed in the lecture given last night by S. R. Stoddard, the famous Adirondack artist, who with a few words of explanation, gave a public exhibition of 225 colored stereopticon views. The lecture was exceedingly interesting, and among the large and representative audience present many assemblymen and senators were noted. . . .

"The 'drowned lands' of the Raquette River valley came in for particular attention because it showed the incalculable damage done by the reckless damming of the streams by the lumbermen. What had once been one of the most beautiful valleys in the Adirondacks is now a scene of malodorous desolation. . . .

"Evidently the lawmakers who saw this program were greatly impressed by it, and it is hoped that it will have a salutary effect on the legislation which will be considered during this session."

The same lecture was repeated in most of the larger cities of the state. Then, on the following May 20th, the long-awaited law was passed. What Stoddard showed had its desired effect.

Naturally, the noted photographer-lecturer did not deserve all the credit for this hard-earned achieve-

16

ment nor did he ever claim it. But it is noteworthy that the Forest Commission, the original Adirondack Park Association and various other organizations and individuals engaged in protecting the Wilderness were quick to acknowledge his valued services.

The lecture series continued until about 1905; then Stoddard embarked upon another venture—the publication of his *Northern Monthly*. This magazine was planned to continue some of the crusading work—but not the frequent, futile, big game restoration schemes—started by the youthful, zestful Harry V. Radford in *Woods and Waters*. The first issue of the *Monthly* came out in May 1907.

The early copies of this full-sized magazine were full of Adirondack articles and his photographs. They contained powerful attacks against the despoliation of the mountains by the lumbering and power interests, against land grabs, pollution and corrupt politicians. He lashed out in vehement opposition to lax enforcement of the game laws.

His special target was the needless and senseless slaughter of humans that cast its pall over every season. It distressed him so that he even advocated hounding the deer, a method outlawed in 1902, if that type of hunting, which he deplored, would save the life of even one man.

Such outspoken, uncompromising opinions won the aging editor (then 64) few friends and many foes, but he never wavered in his avowed principles. The magazine became smaller in size as its circulation shrank. In September 1908, the publisher reluctantly printed the valedictory issue. He died in Glens Falls less than nine years later—April 26, 1917.

Margaret Sidney, better known as the author of the *Three Little Peppers*, also wrote *An Adirondack Cabin* and used Stoddard's photographs as illustrations. In acknowledgement she wrote: "Mr. Stoddard, as is well known, has done more by his pictures and his pen than any other person to open up the great Adirondack wilderness to the notice of the public. And it is due to him to say that the loving enthusiasm he has brought to his work has invested the vast forest with a charm that every intelligent tourist deeply appreciates."

Add to the above testimonial due recognition for his maps, his incomparable illustrated lectures, his hard-hitting editorials for the cause of conservation. Next take into consideration the bulky photographic equipment and supplies of eighty years ago and realize the labor involved in getting all this paraphernalia through the Indian Pass, or into the Colden area and up Marcy. Although the photographer did not travel alone, these trips were anything but Sunday strolls. . . .

A more recent evaluation of Stoddard's place in history was stated by Pieter Fosburgh, former editor of the New York State *Conservationist*, in the June-July 1949 issue of that much-respected magazine:

"Any of a dozen appellations would describe Seneca Ray Stoddard but posterity will know him best as the man who with his bulky, old-fashioned camera and tripod, his glass plates and emulsions captured the Adirondacks. By recording so faithfully and with such feeling the beauty of the North Woods, Stoddard provided a powerful argument for both their protection and their enjoyment. He was a conservationist."

These well-chosen words sum up best the remarkable career of the versatile, incredibly industrious man from Glens Falls.

OLD TIMES IN THE ADIRONDACKS

Being the Narrative of a Trip Into the Wilderness in 1873
by S. R. Stoddard

CHAPTER I

CAPTAIN ROCKWELL AND THE STEAMER VERMONT TRIP

Ring up the curtain to low, sweet music, the music of a September night, the blending of the myriad voices of the swamp into one long monotone, that seems to make you, wherever you stand and listen, its center. The scene is a dark waste of water, up out of which grow reeds and coarse grasses that sway back and forth with the surging waves; over at the west is a low range of bluffs; on the east are mountains. Nearby, dusky white strips run here and there, beyond which a broader one reflects the cloudy sky. Dark bodies are moving slowly along and lights twinkle as they pass to and fro; beyond, and to the south a high hill rises up, belted with strings of stars. At its base they hang in clusters; they separate and pass up and down, are swung in circles, disappear and appear again in a most curious manner, and faintly come the voices of the boatmen, the drivers, the lock-tenders, and the busy hum of the distant village. At the north, where the western wall comes down, the solid rock is notched out, over which rise the rocky crests of a mountain range, while away beyond wind the marsh-bordered rock-hemmed waters of Lake Champlain.

A low, rumbling sound comes from the south. Then the solid wall that shuts us in on that side seems riven asunder, and from out of the earth, with breath of flame, and eye of fire gleaming out ahead, thunders the night express. Across the marsh it comes, bringing in its train a host of lesser lights. With a shriek that clashes sharply and is broken into a confused din of echoes, it plunges into the northern wall, through the narrow cut to the other side. Then with the hiss of escaping steam, the noisy clanging of its bell, the rattling of iron rods and links, the trembling, jerking and swaying of the long coaches, the brakes are drawn hard against the moving wheels. Then with the dying roar of its subsiding power, the iron monster rests at the end of its journey.

Just for the moment we felt the hush
"—the rest of the tide between the ebb and the flow"——then the nature of the sounds change. The quick, sharp words of command, of shouting and confusion, the shuffling of feet, as streams of life pour out from the various coaches, and converging, flow over the broad plank onto the boat that has been waiting to receive them. There is no need of asking the way; it is plain to all, for while on the left is nothing but darkness and a dingy, uninviting pile of buildings, on the right raises a great mass of white, with moving forms and flashing light; windows bright, with stained glass and frosted silver, rising tier on tier, begirt with beams and rods of iron, and above all, coming up from the fires below, wave banners of flame, whose fiery particles separating, dance away and are lost in the darkness. Whew! What a storm, not a thunder storm exactly, although there are indications of the sulphurous in the language sometimes heard, but a shower of baggage. It rains trunks, boxes, satchels, bundles, bags, from the car which has been brought to a stop directly in front of the gang-plank, and a

double stream of trucks, drawn and propelled by stalwart men, go down under huge loads, and, coming up empty, run and wheel and dodge about, appearing always on the point of, but never actually getting run over.

Through all the confusion the man who seems to have the least to do stands quietly by the rail, seeing everything, but saying nothing, unless occasionally to give a command in a low tone. Then, as the last truck load is on the move, he touches a cord at his hand, a bell up in the pilot house tinkles, a few quick strokes on the big bell follow, the last man rushes over the plank, which is pulled aboard, and the great hawsers are cast off. Again, the little bell up where the pilot stands signifies that the boat is from thence out under his control, and he is responsible for her safety. Now, down along the wires to the engine room the message goes; we hear the long hollow breathing of the steam as it rushes into the cylinder; the ponderous beam above tips slowly on its center; the wheels seem stepping on the water as they revolve; the great mass swings out into the channel, and moves away through the night like a great pearl surrounded by a luminous atmosphere. A little shining world all alone by itself.

Thus we saw it one night in the autumn of '73. *We* means the Professor and myself. Who the Professor is, or what he professes, doesn't matter, as long as this is a non-professional trip; but it may be of interest considering the field selected for our observations to know that the Professor is not actually stupendous, either in length, breadth or thickness, and not particular about his diet; perish the thought! He simply abstains from the absorption of that mysterious compound known as hash, on account of the uncertainty of its origin. Revolts at sight of sausages, as it is unpleasantly suggestive of a dear little dog that he once loved. Can't endure cream in his coffee, because it "looks so, floating round on top," and whose heart bleeds and appetite vanishes if an unlucky fly chances to take a hot bath in his tea. To these peculiarities, add a disposition to see the fun in his own forlornness, and with boyishness dyed in the wool, the Professor stands before you. As for the author of this, perhaps the least said the better. He hasn't the heart to say anything bad, and a determination to confine himself strictly to facts interferes somewhat with the glowing eulogy struggling to find vent; suffice it to say, that nature was very lavish in the bestowal of longitude, although not noticeably so in regard to latitude, giving also a disposition to dare, and a physical development capable of enduring a vast amount of arduous rest. Going—the dainty Professor and the ease-loving writer, enthusiastic sportsmen, with neither gun, rod, umbrella or other instrument of death, armed only with sketch and note-book, and hearts to drink in the glories of the great wild woods—to the mountains for health and strength to frames not over-strong.

Steamer Vermont II

We found ourselves on board the "Vermont," the largest of the Champlain steamers; and as it swung out into the channel, went out forward, up odd little pieces of stairway and canvas side hills; ducked under and climbed over iron rods and groped along in the darkness on the hurricane deck to the pilot-house.

As we entered, our eyes becoming accustomed to the darkness, made out the form of Rockwell, the chief pilot, with two assistants, wrestling with the many-spoked wheel, which throbbed and trembled as they forced it over to one side, while the lights ahead seemed to swing swiftly past as we swept around a sharp bend in the channel.

A quick, low word of command, and the chain rattled and the wheel spun around like lightning as they jumped away from it.

"Now," said the pilot.

Six hands pattered on the polished spokes, and the air seemed full of clawing, jumping shadows.

"Over with her."

The wheel creaked and snapped with the strain brought to bear on it; the lights away out ahead, that had passed across to the right, now raced wildly back to the left, and we circled around in the darkness, out of which, into the circle of light that surrounded us, came reedy shores and low lines of bushes, seeming almost to brush against us as we passed.

"Steady now. Good evening, gentlemen."

The last half of the sentence, while it was friendly, was evidently intended as a sort of reconnaissance. It had inquiry in it, and said plainly, "I want to hear the sound of your voice."

We said, "Good evening."

"Up a little—I know your voice—steady—let me see—let her run—Oh, yes, I remember now," and he greeted me cordially by name. "I saw you—hold her there—last summer. You came up here, and this other gentleman was with you. I didn't recognize your voice at first—hard over; that light's out again—you are a little hoarse; you ought to take something for that."

"We are; a trip to the mountains."

He said, "It is an excellent plan to—crowd her against the bank there let her chaw the re-action will clear her wished he could luff a point boys——pass his life among the grand things——hug the shore a little closer and look through nature up to nature's wind a little flawy, and she's down at the head. Then he sandwiched Beecher between Susan B. Anthony and Victoria C. Woodhull; said she was light aft, and clawed to starboard; asked if we could fully indorse Professor Tyndall's theory of nebular hegira; ruined the reputation of Andromeda and Cassiopeia and other heavenly bodies by hopelessly entangling them with Butler and Massachusetts politics. Thought the Greek slave a perfect figure; said she sucked mud through here sometimes, and they had to be careful of her flues. Wanted to know if we had given the evolvement of solar faculae much thought; descended with Darwin to our remote progenitors; gyrated among the wheeling constellations; floated awhile through eternity; touched on the creation; paddled around with Noah; got lost with the children of Israel; skittered along down through the Dark Ages; said it wasn't going to rain; which suggested Sodom and Gomorrah and Lot's wife; wondered how many the Shah averaged, and thought he was no such man as the ridiculously proper Joseph. Admired Joan of Arc—said she carried an awful head of steam; but her boilers were good, undoubtedly, or Mr. Root would have made a fuss about it. Then he wanted our opinion as to the probable origin of creative energy and of the cohesive materialism of latent force.

Shades of Egypt! the Professor wilted and we had to admit that Moses himself couldn't get us out of the scientific wilderness, and Rockwell thought Moses wasn't much of a pilot any way. And speaking of military men, he said, "Phil Sheridan is a brick; just as full of fun as an egg of meat." He tells the following, which the General himself related when he, with the President and family, passed through the lake in 1872. They were at the "Thousand Islands," when one day Sheridan wandered off alone and came across an old farmer, with whom he entered into conversation, and ended by offering him a drink from his brandy flask. The old fellow took a generous draught and, when pressed, even a second. Then, as the General was leaving, he suddenly bethought himself that he would like to know who it was that carried such good liquor. "Who be ye?" said he. "Who've I had the honor of drinking with?"

"My name's Sheridan." said the General. "No, *be* it though; ye ain't any relation to *Gineral* Sheridan, be ye?"

"Well, rather. *I'm* General Sheridan!"

"Ye *ain't though*," said the old farmer, who had a profound reverence for the hero of Winchester, whom he considered the greatest man living, hardly able to believe that he understood aright, "hev I been drinking with Gineral Sheridan himself?"

"Yes, sir," said Little Phil, pompously straightening up and enjoying the effects of his words, "You have had the honor of a drink out of General Philip Sheridan's own brandy flask."

The old chap gazed at the short, thick-set form before him, then a "sold" expression came over him, and his look of blended wonder and reverence changed to disgust as he growled out, "Not — by — a — damn — site — little — feller — Gineral — Sheridan's over — seven — feet — high."

Phil left, feeling that he had tried to pass himself off for a great man, and had been caught in the act.

Chapter II

The Noble Red Man—Arrival at Port Kent

Thus, the pilot mixed art, science, physics and navigation together; with an eye that never relaxed its vigilant watch out ahead, peering into the darkness, seeming to feel rather than see the channel; now shunning a dusky mass that proved to be solid shore when it comes within our circle of light, anon plunging into a deep abyss of darkness, apparently right into the mountain-side, whose shadowy form danced away as the eye sought to fix its outline. Twisting about, now to the right, now to the left, now circling around a lamp hung out as a guide, then away toward others that seemed passing and repassing each other, as the boat swayed to and fro, never touching, although in places a deviation the width of the boat to the right or left would have brought it on the muddy banks. It crept onward through the night, at times seeming to hang out over the reeds; anon, waking a whole swarm of hissing, chuckling echoes as we ran close under a rocky wall. Through the narrow west channel it went, out across a dusky plane of light, to touch at a lonely-looking dock; then onward into broader strips of water and under the frowning promontory of Ticonderoga. Then we went below.

Here, on the main deck, which on shore would be the reception-room or general office, as the night advanced, was to be found a motley gathering of all grades and degrees. Some were doubled up on the seats which ran along the sides and down through the middle, where, with mouths opened and hats tipped jauntily down over musical noses, they were enjoying a blissful repose. Others indicated their right to wear bristles by occupying two or three compartments of the same, and working themselves into a terribly chaotic state by limp attempts to accommodate their forms to the alternate soft cushions and iron arms which separated them. Here lounged a jabbering group of laborers, probably destined to operate at some point on the New York and Canada railway, now being built along the west shore, and there on the floor, where it was necessary to step over or among them, to pass, was

"Lo! The Poor Indian."
(Shortfellow.)
Should you ask me of this people,
Saying, who are these that gather
By themselves, and lying, slumber
In the night-time and the gang-way,
I should answer, I should tell you:

'Tis the children of the forest,
'Tis the mighty Indian nation.
Stealing, like the silent Arab,
Stealing,—for it is their nature,—
To their gracious queen's dominion,
From some giddy haunt of fashion
Where they pitched their birchen wigwam,
Made of hemlock boards and bed-quilts,
And "pursued the gentle calling
Practiced by the gentle savage,"

Sleeping days, and nightly prowling
Where the laden clothes-line flappeth,
And the timid chicken roosteth.

See that untaught child of nature
With the proud and kingly bearing,
With a heart that knows not terror,
Wrap his raglan close around him.
Sleeps—and like an untamed porker,
Kicks and snorts in native freedom;
Heir to all the land about him
With the proof upon his person.
Fearing naught but soap and water
That might take his birthright from him.

See! the mother of her people
Sleeps the sleep of sweet contentment,
With her nose and toes upturning
And her native snore uprising
With its wild reverberations
Through the snags of yellow ivory
Like the winds of ocean raving
'Mong the reefs and crags chaotic
Of some wave-washed reeking cavern;
Or the wild tornado sweeping,
Through the lightning-riven hemlock.

See the dusky Indian maidens,
Graceful as the bending willow,
Sprawling 'round among the warriors,
Mingling with the dogs promiscuous,
With an air of free abandon
And of comfort, quite refreshing;
See! with modesty retiring,
From the rude gaze of the public,
They have drawn their scanty clothing
Close about their lovely faces,

Thus to hide their tender blushes.
Length we see was not essential
To the fashion of their garments;
Not voluminous their raiment
Nor elastic in its nature,
And in truth the pictured story
Is at least unique and novel,
For when drawn above their faces
It must lack in other places.

    Thus they gather, gather, gather;
In the night-time and the gang-way,
Old and young and middle-aged,
Squaw and Papoose, Dog and Warrior,
Interlaced and intermingled
Like the fish-worms in a bait-box,
Human hash of doubtful gender,
Dream of chaos, radiating
    Legs and arms and sounds mysterious,
    Come of contact with the pale-face.

Lo the poor Indian! (Stoddard drawing)

Lo! the poor but honest Ingin,
With his dark eye full of sadness,
Full of rayless, hopeless longing,
Gazing backward, ever backward
To that happy time now vanished,
When he wandered o'er the prairie,
O'er the mountain and the fenland,
Through the dark and tangled wildwood,
Free as bird or winds of ocean
Or the scurrying mists of cloudland,
Drifting, drifting, flitting, passing
Out upon that boundless ocean,
To the unknown, the hereafter,
Vanishing before the pale-face,
Melting like the fleeting sour-
Kraut before a famished Dutchman.

Sic transit gloria mundi.
Hic illae lacrymae.

Jupiter was high up in the east, shining like a young moon, and faint signs of coming day were apparent when we left the steamer and passing into the shadow of that architectural triumph on the dock at Port Kent, got into the waiting stage and set out for Keeseville. Climbing the hill a ride of three miles over what we took to be a "corduroy," but which we were informed was the remains of a plank-road, brought us to Birmingham Falls at the head of Ausable Chasm. Here the Professor and I alighted on the steps of the hotel while the stage proceeded on its way to Keeseville, a little more than a mile distant.

Chasm House, Birmingham Falls

The Chasm House is one of those large, comfortable-looking old stone houses with generous apartments, great roomy window seats and an air of substantial home comfort about it not often found in hotels. It was build for a private residence and altered to accommodate travelers when the growing interest felt in the Chasm demanded a place of entertainment. Having accommodations for about 20 guests, it is a very pleasant, quiet place to stop at. The proprietor, H. H. Bromley, is a jolly, easy-going sort of fellow, ever ready to devote himself to his guests, not seeming to own himself when they are around, and withal a pleasant companion on the various excursions to be taken from his house. Soon a shuffling sound was heard within, a light appeared in the hall, the door was thrown open, and there, with hair awry, one eye half open, and arrayed in a partially adjusted pair of pants, with wonder on his phiz and a lamp in his hand, stood the proprietor. "Well-by-thunder," he remarked by way of greeting, recognizing one of his visitors. Then his six-foot-form assumed the appearance of a wet rag as he dropped back and apparently hung himself up against the door-post while he went through the form of an ecstatic laugh without the slightest sound escaping his lips. We couldn't see anything funny, and I don't think he had the least particle of an idea of what he was laughing at, but he seemed to drop off into a laugh, simply because it required less exertion than to keep sober. Then we went inside, our host foraged around for pillows and blankets and retired to his bed once more, while we curled down on a pair of sofas, getting another night's rest and rising refreshed to partake of a late breakfast and to do the wonderful Ausable Chasm.

Chapter III

Ausable Chasm.

A little depression in the otherwise level country, a wooded valley with gently sloping sides, marks the site of this grand wonder—a Yosemite in miniature almost at the doors of the great city, and curiously enough, comparatively unknown. The river flowing quietly along the valley from the south and west, passes Keeseville, plunges over Alice Falls, square against a solid wall of rock, turns at right angles and, wheeling around in confused swirls, now right, now left, falls in a mass of foam over the rocks at Birmingham, then hurrying downward between towering cliffs and over rocks where the sun never shines, emerges from the gloom out into the glorious sunlight, and onward to mingle with the muddy waters of Lake Champlain.

This freak of nature is not alone of its kind, but one of a system of rents in the earth's surface that probably extend all over the northern portion of the State, the most noticeable of the others being at Chateaugay Falls; on the Opalescent, and higher up on the east and west branches of the Ausable. Neither are we to say how or when they were formed. The walls that now are from ten to fifty feet apart were undoubtedly sometime united and solid. Projections on the one hand are often faced by corresponding depressions on the other; layers of rock on one side duplicated on the other. Prof. Emmons, State Geologist, found here petrified specimens of the lowest or first orders of animal life, and ripple marks made when the rock was in its plastic state. Above these, in successive layers, towers seventy feet of solid rock.

Until recently there had been but little done to open the Chasm to the comfortable inspection of the public. Some parts had probably never been visited, and there were but two or three places where it was considered safe to climb down into the gorge. However, in 1873, a company of Philadelphians secured nearly all the land surrounding, have commenced the erection of a hotel nearby, and built stairways, galleries and bridges so that nearly the entire length can now be traversed with comfort, the remainder in a boat.

Passing through the "Lodge"—the Professor, Bromley and I—and descending by a stairway of 125 steps to the bottom, we passed up into the spray from the cataract, which, divided in the center, falls in almost unbroken sheets a distance of seventy feet, hurries northward to the Horseshoe Falls, passing over which it butts squarely against the wall at the Elbow, and turning to the east goes swiftly onward in its narrow, tortuous channel.

The cave known as the "Devil's Oven" is a hole in the rock about thirty feet deep by twenty high, which we entered, feeling that it would be no harm to get accustomed to the thing, as there is a good deal of uncertainty concerning the future. We found it much more comfortable than the name would lead one to expect. And here let me remark that his satanic majesty seems to own considerable real estate in the place, claiming, besides the "Oven," a "Pulpit," "Easy Chair," "Anvil," "Stairway" and, of *course*, a "Punch

Bowl." Here, at the left, the waters break through "Hell Gate" into the eddy called the "Punch Bowl." Just above the "Oven" a light bridge of the "Mystic Gorge," a crevice leading off at right angles with the main fissure toward the north and continued in a similar opening on the south.

Ausable Chasm Hell's Gate

"What is that called?" I asked, alluding to a huge rock that towered up almost over our heads, across the Chasm. Bromley scratched his head and regretted that he had been unable to find a name for it yet. Poor fellow! he has approaching baldness, caused by frequent attempts to dig out appropriate and nice-sounding names for the many objects of interest near-by. "Call it Moses," suggested the Professor, and "Moses" it was christened by unanimous consent.

"Who was Moses?" The question was asked soberly, and a quiet individual who had joined us, with a book in his hand and a semi-ministerial hang to his clothes, proceeded to tell us in good faith, as he supposed the question was asked by an anxious inquirer after knowledge. How insignificant we felt looking up at the strip of blue sky, the great river walls and the dark tower of rocks above us—"henceforth shall you be called Moses; fit emblem of thy namesake who stood face to face with the great Creator amidst the thunderings of Mount Sinai."

A little farther on the gallery runs along half way up the almost perpendicular side of the Chasm, around "Point of Rocks" to the "Smugglers' Pass," nearly opposite which is "Howe's Cave," along past the "Post Office," suggested by the honey-combed rock at the side showing deposits made by the water in times of floods thirty feet above its present level, then over and down on "Table Rock." Here they end, and stepping into a boat we can be set over—we can almost jump across—and stand under the "Sentinel" and "Cathedral Rocks," and if we choose, find our way up through one of the cracks in them to the light above. Curious in their formation, seeming as though they had been sliced off and held from falling by their connection with the parent rock at their backs. The "Anvil" at their base bears a striking resemblance to that for which it was named. Above, the river bends slightly to the right, and is soon hidden from view, the walls jagged and rough on the left while to the right the hemlocks cling, and dripping, slimy mosses hang downward.

Now for some way down (I could not judge of the distance, for the senses seemed overwhelmed with the grandeur of the scene) the water runs straight away, shut in by walls reaching perpendicularly up, and so near together that it seems as though you could almost leap across from one to the other, then turns squarely again toward the north. We stepped into the little flat-bottomed boat, and Bromley, seizing the paddle like the grim ferryman of the Styx, with one of his silent though hearty laughs pushed out into the stream. The swift water caught us and we were whirled onward, under the great walls, and carried swiftly down the stream. Once, where the water scooped downward over a rock and then curled over, as if trying to climb backward upon itself, it came in over the sides, wetting us slightly. But we passed onward into the lower gateway, where the water piled up in the centre, and lifted us like cork on molten lead; then out into the eddy under the protecting point, whence we climbed up out of the depths to the surface of the earth, glad to get out into the clear sunlight once more. We had left the world above, descended to "Hell Gate," cooled off in the "Devil's Oven," ascended and descended "Jacob's Ladder" in anything but an Angelic state of perspiration, moralized over Moses, wondered what mystery there was about the mystic forge, scrambled mildly past "Point Surprise," gazed reverently up at the "Devil's Pulpit," ran the "Sentinel," and after a tempestuous voyage in a gallant scow, effected a masterly landing, and were glad to get out. For while we felt that it was good to be there where we realized our own insignificance, it came to be oppressive at last, and we felt with Will Carleton that "To appreciate Heaven well—It is good for a man to have some fifteen minutes of Hell."

If unwilling to take the boat ride, which is ordinarily perfectly safe, you can ascend the old stairway in "Cathedral Rocks" to the level above, where the carriages meet those who do not wish to return through the Chasm and where refreshments can be procured if desired.

Chapter IV

Keeseville—Au Sable—Wilmington

The Nail Rod Works, on the road between Keeseville and the Chasm, are also well worth a visit. See that mass of iron as it is brought from the furnace door, glowing with heat, scintillating and spluttering like a young Fourth of July; the tongs which grasp this lump of fire are suspended by a chain from a wheel which runs along the iron track overhead. Now it is swung around under the great trip-hammer which descends, softly at first then swifter as the glowing loop shrinks down weeping tears of blood. Another heat and it is passed through between iron rollers having grooves of various sizes running around, through the largest first, then a size smaller, and this repeated until it gets too cold to work or is as required.

Once more they come from the furnaces, glowing red, and as the flat bars pass through the last set of rollers it comes forth nearly round. Now it is passed rapidly through, back and forth, each time lengthening out farther than before, and as it is constantly forced along it writhes and squirms about on the black floor like a serpent of fire—a string of red-hot iron seventy to eighty feet in length. This is nail rod.

Now cut into convenient lengths, it is passed to the several workmen, who, heating it in small furnaces, feed it to the curious little machines in front of them, which, eating red-hot iron, drop finished nails like the ticking of a watch.

Ausable Chasm Horse Nail Works

The Ausable Horse Nail Company was organized in 1862 with a capital stock of $80,000. Now, the shares are valued at fabulous prices due, it would seem, to the company's possession of the right to use the little machines by which the nails are shaped, the invention of Daniel Dodge who, unlike most inventors, has made money out of it. Here they have over fifty of the little machines in operation, capable of turning out 150 pounds each, finished nails per day, 100 nails to the pound and worth, on an average, twenty-four cents per pound.

At Keeseville we dropped in on our genial, eccentric old friend Lansing, of the *Republican,* for information; because editors know all about everything, and, as they don't have to work it relieves the monotony of their idle life by allowing them to contribute something for the benefit of anxious seekers after knowledge. Keeseville is situated on the Ausable River, about five miles from its mouth, and is a thoroughly wide-awake little village; not set upon a hill, actually, but rather the reverse, and a person wading across the sandy plain on either side will be surprised when he reaches the front of the hill to see so much life and business in the hollow below. The water-power is immense, and utilized by the twine, wire and horse-nail manufacturers—the latter being the principal industry of the town. There are also several elegant private residences, churches and stores, built of Potsdam sandstone, which here abounds.

Leaving Keeseville, our road followed along up the valley of the Ausable, through fertile farming country that gradually gave place to a wilder and more broken district; while the river grew rapid and the hills along its shore became rocky and precipitous. Clintonville, with its said-to-be largest forge on the continent, and decayed, ashy, sooty look, was passed as was "Point-of-Rocks," the southern terminus of the Plattsburgh Railroad. At Ausable Forks, (which also bore unmistakable signs of being a coal-handling town), we left the regular stage route, and climbing to a sandy plateau west of the village, picked our way through a forest of stunted pines, choosing our road from a multitude that seemed to cover and run in every direction across it. Three miles of this sandy way through the woods and we came out on the western slope, in full view of the towering form of "Old Whiteface," and—through Wilmington Notch—the blue of the more distant ranges. Then down into the valley we went, and up along the rapid Ausable to where we struck the stage road once more, having saved over two miles by our cut through the woods. Our driver seemed much interested in mill privileges, talking *dam* to his horses a good share of the time. When we inquired if he was a Christian, he dodged the question and remarked something about a dam in California. Then he pointed out the ruins of an old forge and said somebody dammed the river there once. This horrified the Professor, but he soon recovered sufficiently to intimate that it didn't look worth a dam to him, and thought that if it was true it was damned bad.

At last we entered the little hamlet of Wilmington and drew up in front of the hotel—not a very elegant affair, to be sure; but we felt at home as soon as we caught sight of the big, honest, square-looking fellow with his pants in his boots and fun in his clear blue eyes, who came out to meet us. We inquired if he was the landlord.

"Well, I don't know," said he, with a glance down at his working clothes; "it's been so long since we had any company that it don't pay to keep a landlord." Then he continued sadly: "The season's about over, I guess, for you're the first travelers we've seen in a week." Then he took us inside, built up a rousing fire, and in a short time gave us a dinner that could not fail to satisfy the most fastidious.

Wilmington in 1873

Wilmington, aside from the hotel, has a deserted, worn-out sort of look, and while it appears to possess a little of everything it seems as though nothing ever came to a head. Two or three shut-up-looking churches—Methodist, Presbyterian and Lutheran—a few scattered houses, an old forge, saw, starch and grist mills, all having a decidedly dead appearance. The place was owned a long time ago by one Major Sanford, who came here, built two or three stills, and went to making whiskey. "Those were the times when it wasn't a sin to make it. They didn't put in as much poison as they do nowadays," said my informant. "Well, he went to making whiskey, built mills and that brick church and then failed. Then George Weston came here with $10,000, cut a road to the top of the mountain and built a little house up there. He soon lost all *his* money and sold out to Sidney Weston, of Winooski, Vermont, who is smart as lightning and will make it pay if any living man can."

Chapter V

Whiteface Mountain—The Ascent—Little Footprints—Thanks Be To God For The Mountains.

Cut off from its kindred on the south by Wilmington Notch, and on the north by one almost as deep, pyramidal in form, although somewhat the longest north and south, its base clothed in inky spruce and balsams, its naked granite head among the clouds "Old Whiteface" stands, one of the finest mountain peaks in the Adirondacks.

"I'll tell you what I'll do," said our warm-hearted landlord as we sat that night discussing the ascent of "Old Whiteface," "If you will stay over I will take you two miles up the mountain—as far as we can conveniently get with a wagon—and send a guide to the top with you. It's the grandest mountain view to be had in the Adirondacks, and I don't want you to go away without seeing it." Of course we accepted, only insisting that he go with us.

At 9 o'clock the next morning, with the thermometer at 48, we set out up the mountain. Two miles from the hotel we left the wagon, which returned to the hotel with instructions to meet us at sunset, and proceeded up the bridle path toward the summit, traveling about a mile westerly; then, turning toward the south, entered the standing timber and began the as-

Whiteface Mountain—Three Braves

cent in earnest.

At the end of a half hour we had gone another mile and came out on an open space called "Lookout Point," half way to the top. Here the blueberries grew thick, and we scraped whole handfuls from the bushes and ate them, gathering in ten minutes all we cared for, then resumed our course and pressed upward through the dark woods, scrambling up the steep path where great rocks alternated with pools of black muck in a semi-liquid state, trodden and mixed by horses' feet. We wondered that horses could climb such places with a hundred and fifty to two hundred pounds of humanity on their backs. But Baldwin said to his knowledge not an accident, further than being lost for a night, ever happened on the mountain. We reached the shanty, three-fourths of a mile from the summit, a little past noon, and here occurred a desperate encounter between hungry men and uncounted slices of bread and butter, supported by other fixtures.

The shanty is in a small clearing, at the highest point where wood and water can be obtained. It has log sides with a roof, part canvas and part bark. Within is a parlor cook stove. Along one side, raised a little above the floor was a platform that looked as though it might do service as Brigham Young's family bedstead, covered with spruce and hemlock branches and blankets. A sort of cross between a stairway and ladder led up to the ladies' dormitory under the sharp roof, through which the stars could peep in places. Here, in the bed which covered nearly the entire floor, we discovered signs of the tender feeling with which the fair sex was regarded, in the springy moss and fine tips that had been stripped from the larger branches on which the lords of creation slept down below. The pipe from the stove in the lower room, where a fire could be kept roaring all night, passed up through this upper room and made it comfortable in the coldest weather. Altogether it was a cozy, jolly, fun-provoking place to be in where, as our guide remarked, "if there was any fun in a fellow it was going to show itself." We, in imitation of others before us who had written their names in every reachable place in the building, registered and proceeded on our way to the summit.

"Pretty rough work," said Baldwin, "but hundreds of people come up every year and ride clear to the top. A big doctor came here from Buffalo with his family and a very valuable four-horse team that he had been all over the country with. When he said he was going to the top of the mountain with them, I tried to stop him, and I offered to get horses that were accustomed to the road for nothing, rather than have him hurt his. But no, 'Other horses have been there, have they not?' said he, and when I told him yes, he said, 'Then mine can go.' So he took them out of the harness and put his wife, a woman that would weigh two hundred, on the fieriest one of the lot and started. I felt bad for I *knew* something would happen. They rode those horses to the very top and just turned around and"—. We gazed down over the fearful precipice at our feet while our hearts seemed to cease their motion as he slowly concluded—"and rode down again!"

"How can ladies manage to keep on the horses' backs, where it seems almost impossible for the horse to get along alone?"

"*Manage!*" said he, "like a man, of course! It makes me laugh to see them sometimes when they find that they've got to go that way. So modest when they start—some of them. They are dreadfully afraid of showing their *feet* at first, but they soon get over that and come down with colors flying, I tell you. I don't know as they would ever have done it if Mrs. Murray—wife of the Rev. Adirondack Murray—hadn't set the fashion. She's a dashing, independent sort of a woman, who don't let thoughts of what people may say interfere with her plans. Well! After Mrs. Murray set the example, we had no difficulty. Now lots of them go up that way. With the horses we have, and a guide at their side, there is not the slightest danger."

We had noticed, all the way up, fresh tracks, made by three separate persons—one, a man's, which also appeared to have descended later, and two evidently made by ladies, one short and thick, the other slender, and dainty in its manner of touching the ground. It had been a matter of wonderment to us, and "Little Foot-prints," as we styled the owner of the dainty stepping foot, was a constantly recurring subject of speculation. "Where is Little Foot-prints? Who is she? Is she pretty?—Of course! And the other— why are they apparently alone? Why has the Big Foot gone back?" Questions we hoped soon to solve; questions that preyed upon the Professor, as the oft-twirled moustache and passage of his fingers through his auburn locks would seem to indicate. Of course it was nothing to me, and only out of mere curiosity that I managed to reach the top first. But—where was Little Foot-prints? Not there, for the summit, the sides, the backbone of the mountain up over which we had passed, were primeval, unyielding rock. They had not returned by the path! They may have gone down the sides in some other direction, but the feeling took possession of us that our "Little Foot-prints" had taken wings and flown up among the angels just a little higher than where we stood.

How can I describe it?—The wonderful beauty of the day, the clear, crisp atmosphere surrounding us— the great purple-rimmed basin, in the center of which, lifted up on a pinnacle, we stood, while the mighty, sweeping dome of heaven came down all around and blended with the mountain edges. A keen, wintry blast sweeping past, penetrating even through the heavy blankets that we had brought from the house below. The land was frozen nearly as hard as the rock on which it rested. Every stunted bush, every blade of coarse grass which clung to the wind-swept summit was gleaming with frost needles and sparkling like spun glass in the bright sunshine. Below, the country lay spread out in the glory of its autumn dress, in gold and crimson, brown and green; in pearly lakes and threads of silver, in purple hills and mellow distance, and over all lay a mantle of tender blue haze, seen only in autumn. Not smoke, but something that suggests the myriad millions of pale, sweet ghosts of falling leaves and dying flowers. Back toward the north ran the sharp ridge up which we had toiled, naked and dark for a quarter of a mile, then a stunted growth of balsams gnarled and twisted; a few live branches low down at the surface, the tops dead and dry. Then, as we look further the spruce and cedar, dark and thick down to the belts of birches and maples below. Away off to the east is Lake Champlain, lost in the mist toward the north, shut in by the Green Mountains beyond; still farther the White Hills of old New England. To the south are the Great Peaks: Haystack, Marcy—(the cloud-piercer of the Indians), Colden, with the white track of the avalanche down its side; a long line of giants, their dark blue crests rising like ocean billows, grand and changeless in their mighty forms, overwhelming in their sublimity.

Toward the west a lower set of mountain waves are seen—a comparatively level tract of country, cut and lined with a confused network of ponds and streams, with here and there a broad, shining sheet of water. Lake Placid seems at our feet. The Saranacs and Big Tupper farther away, while over the purple rocky rim of the mountains to the north stretched the faint blue of the level Canadas, through which was the silvery gleam of the mighty St. Lawrence.

Turning once more toward grand Indian Pass we see the fields of North Elba, and—a mere speck—the home and last resting place of old John Brown. From the pass above, the Ausable rises and comes toward us. Here and there we catch glimpses of it like a mere thread. Through Wilmington Notch, under the great wall, through the natural flume at our feet it flows past the little village and away to Keeseville, beyond which it plunges down over the rocks at Birmingham, and finds its way out through the dark Chasm to Lake Champlain.

Seventy years ago an avalanche of loose stones and the gathered moss and vegetable deposit of ages went down the western slope of this mountain and the exposed surface, whiter than the rest, is said to have given it the name. There is a more reasonable theory that the old giant's naked brow covered for so long a period with snow, suggested the name of "Whiteface."

Whiteface Mountain—Three Braves at summit (Stoddard drawing)

On the topmost point, firmly attached to the rock, we found the card of the chief of the Adirondack Survey, a metallic disk with this inscription: "Whiteface Mountain, Station No. 2. Verplanck Colvin, S. N. Y. Adirondack Survey, 1872." The surface of the rock was scarred and chiseled with the names of former visitors while as if to rebuke the frivolity of such little thoughts, stretching far across the level, cut deep and clear, were the words, "Thanks be to God for the Mountains!" and every heart joined with that grand old mountain peak in the thought.

The summit is a great, dark, lichen-covered, chaotic mass of broken rock.

From the north and south the ascent is gradual, but on either side it is almost perpendicular for many feet, then curves outward and is covered by the dark evergreens. We gazed down from the dizzy height,

"We heard the troubled flow
Of the dark olive depths of pines, resounding
A thousand feet below."

We marked our homeward course for the days to come through the glistening lakes, away around the blue, serrated summit of Mount Seward, then started on the descent. A sudden exclamation from our guide brought us to his side, to find him inspecting what we took to be the track of a naked foot.

"What is it?"

"A bar—been here since we went up—going down, probably, to the blueberry patch. We may see him if we go careful."

Carefully and expectantly we went, following the track along out to the blueberry patch, but there we lost it. We waited, watched and ate berries until the shadow of the mountain, like a great pyramid reached out and touched the little village, then we resumed our downward way.

"Maybe you'd better lead," said Baldwin, making

a desperate effort to keep his feet from getting the advantage of him, while an ax, tin pail and sundry other articles jingled and thumped about his sides. "It bothers me to have folks treading on my heels." So lead we did. The result may be inferred from a remark Baldwin was overheard to make that night, to the effect that it beat somethin'-or-other how them fellows came down that mountain, "and when I'd get some ways behind and drop into a little dog-trot to catch up, I'd hear that little fellow snicker and away they'd go hell-e-ty-split and I do believe that that long-legged one would cover six feet at a step.' "

Chapter VI

"On The Road"—Att. Clyne—Wilmington Pass.

The morning following our ascent Old White-face had draped his shoulders in a mantle of mist, modestly hiding his face in the clouds, and although the sun came out toward noon and the clouds went scurrying across the sky like a routed army before the advance of an enemy, a legion still hung around his iron head, skulked in the rents and hollows of his furrowed side and crowded close under the lee of his protecting form. It was interesting to watch this vast host—this white-robed army of the sky—maneuvering to gain a place of safety from the fierce west winds which tore it into fragments and strung it to shreds, and rolled it up into great balls to be dashed against the mountain, and separating, pass on either side to wheel into line beyond. Or, caught in the surface current that came up the steep from the west to shoot out over the sharp crest and curl downward into the billowy mass below, where it clung like some tattered signal of distress, its ragged, wind-whipped end stretching away out toward the east.

After dinner we took a carriage, sandwiched Att. Clyne, the driver, between us and started for North Elba. Att. was a pleasant young fellow, who had rather hear or tell a good story than to eat, and that is saying a good deal—for him. He inaugurated a series by telling of the wonderful speed of the particular beast behind which we were riding, the truth of which he would demonstrate when we arrived at a suitable piece of road. We never came to that suitable piece. Once we thought we had, and he encouraged the beast with the whip. She felt encouraged for about ten feet, then rested while we got out and strapped a couple of pieces of whiffletree together which we discovered dangling at her feet, then went ahead again carefully. About two miles south of Wilmington is the "Flume," a furrow in the mountain as the track of a giant plowshare, through which the water shoots like a flash of light. Our road led up along the river, now flashing out abroad in the sunlight as it ripped over the stones, now quiet, then plunging over the "Big Falls" seemed to lose itself in the cavernous depths below.

Wilmington Pass is the natural gateway to North Elba from the north. It is one of the finest, if not the finest, combination of river, rock and mountain scenery to be found in the Adirondacks. It was especially beautiful as we saw it in its autumn dress, that early October day. The road ran by the river, fringed and canopied by crimson and yellow maples, great, ragged, rough-armed birches, cone-shaped balsam, dainty-limbed tamarack and scarlet-berried mountain ash. The pass seems to have been caused by some mighty power that turning neither to the right nor left, struck this mountain range and passed through and onward, carrying everything before it out on the plain beyond, leaving the broken walls on either side to frown down on the torn rocks below, and, when the tempest raged, to thunder back defiance at each other. Then time covered the rocks with mosses, the floods brought rich offerings and

Wilmington Pass or Notch

dropped them in the bottom-land, trees sprang up and found lodging in the cleft rocks, and now all is covered with nature's mantle. No, not all, for at our left, the naked rock rises straight up, fully five hundred feet, at places even projecting beyond its base and seeming ready to fall as great masses have already fallen, through and around which the road goes, with barely sufficient room to pass between the ragged cliffs and the narrow, swift-running river. Across the river at our right is a narrow fringe of bottom-land trees, then rising, precipice above precipice, and cliff on cliff, is "Old Whiteface," his feet washed by the river, his head still among the clouds, and—. There stands that fast beast out to the full extent of the reins, with the pieces of broken whiffletree, dangling at either side.

"Gr-r-r-roop!" *whack!*

The sound was richly musical and unmistakably African for "Get-up!" We were resting, if you please, in the buggy, right in the middle of the road, the Professor and I rapturously enjoying the lovely scenery and innocently talking about subjects entirely foreign to the situation, while "Att." sat squeezed in between us, holding on to one end of the reins and using some very choice language in regard to the mare who stood out at the other, looking around occasionally to see why some one didn't make a move to get her back where she belonged.

"Gr-r-r-r!" whack!

Letters cannot express it. The nearest approach to it is when some seasick mortal rushes to the vessel's side and attempts vainly to give up his own dinner to the fishes. We got out finally, tied the traces back to the crossbar, put the broken whiffletree in the wagon and sent "Att." forward to make repairs.

"Gr-r-roop!" Whack! (Stoddard drawing)

"Gr-r-roop!" whack!

A pair of sorry-looking objects appeared over the brow of a little knoll behind us, rising slowly as rises the stately ship above the watery horizon, first two pairs of hairy ears, then a pair of venerable heads swaying from side to side, then their entire forms loomed above the sandy horizon, and we looked up through a swaying thicket of legs and straps and wooden bars.

"Camels, by darn!" gasped the Professor excitedly, catching sight of what appeared to be the hump peculiar to the "ship of the desert."

No, not camels, Professor, but ancient specimens of horse architecture; style, gothic, with a tendency toward many gables. And that which you think the hump is a French roof of buffalo skin to protect them, or the harness, or both from the rain. Framed in nature's noblest mold those beasts undoubtedly were; but the party who supplied the flesh was apparently short of material, or else they were clothed in their summer suit. The harness bound them round about suggesting suspicion of a latent fire within that might, if aroused, burst forth and rend straps of an ordinary width, as the lightning shivers the mighty oak. Straps crossed and covered those noble animals until they looked like a railroad map of Massachusetts, and at every crossing was a big patch of buffalo skin. The creatures looked kindly at us, with eyes out of which all coltish frivolity had long since flown. Then their expression changed to one of mild surprise as the wagon gently pressed against them, and they found it easier to trot down the hill than to hold back. As they forged up alongside they stopped. They had evidently been driven by a sewing machine agent or some candidate for office, and thought they must stop for every man they saw. We instantly propounded the following conundrum to the driver:

"Why can't we ride in that extra seat?"

He gave it up at once and we got aboard the buck-board.

"Gr-r-r-roop!" whack!

We were under way! The driver was a good-look-ing fellow, intelligent, well-informed, and decidedly attractive in his way, even if his skin was a few shades darker than regulation and his hair unex-plorable in its kinkiness. We inquired his destination and he told us North Elba. As St. Helena suggests the first Napoleon, so North Elba brings with it the pic-ture of an old man with white hair and flowing white beard, crazy some said, but with wonderful method in his madness. A carpet-bagger in Kansas, where he took an active part in the troubles which in 1856 as-sumed the formidable proportions of a civil war. The "Old Man of Osawatomie," whose presence was marked by dissensions and bloodshed; who urged men on to murder in the name of freedom and read his Bible all the time.

In 1859, with a mere handful of men, he struck the first hard blow at the institution of slavery in the South, that probably, more than the eloquence of all the Phillips and Sumners in the world, tended to precipitate the war by which through rivers of blood, four million slaves went free. He was called "a vi-sionary," "an old fool," but men who have given the subject study say that it was the best organized con-spiracy that ever failed. It reached out over the entire Southern States and the blow struck at Harper's Ferry was to be the signal for a general uprising of the blacks, but he misjudged his timber—and failed.

A fanatic, but who can doubt that he thought him-self ordained of the Most High? Undoubtedly he felt that he was specially called to free and educate the blacks. Here at North Elba he secured a large tract of land to demonstrate his theory, and had established quite a colony. Then, feeling that the time had come, he, with three sons, a son-in-law and a few others who had become converted to his belief—twenty-two in all—played at Harper's Ferry—and lost. The Negroes, to whom they trusted so much, left them to fight it out alone. One son escaped, another was shot dead, and still another lay dying by his side, while the old man fought on. At last when overpowered and compelled to surrender, he locked the secrets he possessed in his breast that his friends might not suffer, and died as he had lived, firm in the faith that in some manner he was the divinely-appointed agent who was to lead his children out of the land of bondage. He murmured not against the people for whom he suffered, who had deserted him in his direst need, but stopped to kiss a little Negro baby on his way to the scaffold, seeming to show by the act, how willingly he laid down his life for them and the cause he had espoused.

Then the body of old John Brown, the convicted murderer, a felon with the mark of the hangman's rope on his neck, was taken down from the gallows and borne through the country whose laws he had transgressed, while bells tolled and cities were draped in mourning for his sake, to his old home among the mountains. He had said: "When I die, bury me by the big rock where I love to sit and read the word of God." And there, one terribly cold day in bleak December, a few who had loved the old man laid his body and covered it up in the frozen ground.

"And his soul goes marching on."

Yes, the spirit of old John Brown goes marching on, and with it, keeping time to the music of the old song, whole armies marched to battle, and with the victory came that for which the old man worked and died.

"Gr-r-r-roop!" whack! Back to the reality of a

darky belaboring a pair of absent-minded and almost absent-bodied horses, and they supremely unconscious of the fact. We ventured to inquire if our driver was one of John Brown's pet lambs, and he with, as Mrs. Partington would say considerable "asparagrass," gave us to understand that he was not.

"He established a colony of blacks up here, didn't he?"

"Yes, sah! But they ain't heah now. We are the only fambly of colo'd folks in town."

"Where are they now?"

"All gone?" "Gr-r-r-roop!" (whack!) "See dat hoss—Gone; nobody knows where."

"Mebbe fifteen or twenty famblies, don't know—didn't think much of 'em."

"Slaves, I suppose, that the old man had run in here from the South?"

"No, sah! Not one—G'lang!"

"Where did he get them?"

"Oh, from New York, mostly, I guess—not much account-Niggers—Gr-r-r-roop! What you 'bout?"

"He was generally considered a fanatic, wasn't he?"

"Sah?"

"You thought him a monomaniac?"

"A—yes, Sah! Ge-long, thah."

"You say they are all gone; what has become of them?"

"Don't know; they couldn't make a livin' heah; too cold for 'em; wan't much used to work, I guess; an' couldn't stan' the kind they got heah. Most of 'em was barbers an' sich, who thought they wouldn't have nothing to do when they come heah, an' after the old man died they couldn't get along noway, so they dug out, some of 'em, an' some of 'em died. An' Gur-r-r-one ole niggah froze to death."

"How was that?"

"Well, he went out huntin' one day in de winteh an' got lost in the woods. He had a compass with him, but when they found him they found where he had sot down on a log and picked his compass to pieces, and then sot there till he froze to death!"

It is a well-known fact that people unused to the woods will become so effectually "turned around" that they will be certain the compass points wrong and even distrust the sun itself if it happens to be in a different position from that which they think it ought to be.

"Dem hosses gettin' kinder tired," continued their master; "don't get along over this road very fast."

We accepted the information with polite incredulity, as is becoming in those to whom an unnoticed fact is first made apparent.

"Been on the road a whole week—"

"Getting from the Forks?" I innocently inquired.

"Oh, no, sah; it's only fifteen miles to 'Sable Forks.' I've been carryin' a young lady 'round to see the country—drivin' them hosses steady for a week—"

"Without feeding? Well, now, I don't wonder they—"

"No, no, Sah! I feed 'em reg'lar, only they run out all summer an' I haven't got the hard feed in 'em yet. They ain't very fat just now, but they's good hosses for all that." Then he whipped up lively for two or three rods past a shanty, where we saw Att. busily engaged on what he was pleased to call a whiffletree, to take the place of the broken one. We bade good-bye to our sable friend and sat down by the river-side to make a sketch of the scene. Feeble and unsatisfactory, perhaps, but a suggestion at least of foaming, sparkling, sun-bright water, dancing along among the stones; great shaggy yellow birches, golden beeches, crimson maples and tangled depths of dark green, while through openings in the trees, the gray cliff showed grand and strong, appearing even greater than itself through the tender blue of the luminous haze that intervened. We all got in behind the fast horse and continued on our way up along the river, through a dark, level tract, almost a swamp, where the balsams grew thick and the trailing moss hung in masses from their branches; then out into the open country, where we saw pleasant homes, well-tilled fields, and the river winding smoothly through grassy meadows.

After a while we came to a place where the houses were a little nearer together than anywhere else along the road, so we called that North Elba. The population is rather thin at the best, and the country to a great extent devoted to grazing and grass growing. Winter seems to be the chief season. It never disappoints them in coming and it is seldom that a year passes when snow is not seen on the mountains nearby in every month excepting August.

Chapter VII

The John Brown Grave and Farm—
A Woman Means Business

North Elba is said to be very healthy, so much so that the only manner of taking off is a habit they have of freezing to death, and when this happens, as is often the case in summer, they do not find it necessary to bury them. But (if Att. is to be believed) they simply lay them away somewhere exposed to the pure balsamic air and, in the course of six or seven weeks, they moss over. John Brown was only covered up as a protection against curiosity hunters, who have a habit of chopping off pieces of fossils and the like, and who have broken off pieces of his tombstone to such an extent that it had to be boxed up to keep enough for directory purposes.

Here at North Elba we struck the post-road, running in a north-westerly direction from Elizabethtown to the Saranac Lakes. Turning to the right we proceeded about a mile in a westerly course to a lane which led off toward the south; there we saw a sign bearing the inscription, "John Brown's Farm, Refreshments if desired," with an index finger, which was probably painted by some admirer of the old man's to indicate his present home. The direction, if followed, would take the traveler several degrees higher than we could hope to get in the Adirondacks.

We followed the lane through a strip of woods, into an open field. With the dusk of a solemn twilight settling down over us, we stood by the great rock that the old man loved so well and by the side of which, at his own request, he was buried.

John Brown's homestead, North Elba

The farm is shut in on all sides by thick forests which, on the south, stretch away in unbroken solitude to Indian Pass and the great peaks of the Adirondacks. It has been purchased by a company at whose head as prime mover stands Kate Field. It is now held as a public park and is annually visited by hundreds who, from curiosity or reverence for the old man, make pilgrimages to their Mecca of fanaticism. The house and outbuildings stand in the open field. Nearby are the "big rock" and grave surrounded by a rough board fence.

As we entered the inclosure a little girl came out to remove the box from the headstone, which it was found necessary to cover to preserve from the destroying hand of the relic-hunter. Unlocking and removing the box, we saw an old-fashioned, time-stained, granite-like stone. The corners were chipped and broken off, and defaced so that in places some of the inscription was entirely gone. The upper half was in the quaint characters of "ye olden time," the lower of a recent date. The face bore the following inscription:

John Brown's grave

"In memory of Capt. John Brown Who Died at New York Sept. Ye 3 1776 in the 42 year of Age."

John Brown, Born May 8, 1800 was executed at Charleston, Va., Dec. 2, 1859."

"Oliver Brown, Born Mar. 9, 1839, was Killed at Harper's Ferry Oct. 17, 1859."

On the back was the following:

"In memory of Frederick son of John and Dianth Brown, Born Dec. 21, 1830 and murdered at Osawatomie, Kansas, Aug. 30, 1856 for his adherence to the cause of Freedom."

"Watson Brown, Born Oct. 7, 1835, was wounded at Harpers Ferry & died Oct. 19, 1859."

The grave was strewn with faded flowers; a florist's leaden cross and crown filled with a sodden mass lay on the little mound, and under it, the body of Old John Brown. Alone! Of his large family not one remained to watch over him, but in their place strangers, who knew less of the old man than we who lived far away. His widow and five children out of his twenty, are still living, it is said, scattered over the West, some of them in far-away California.

The stone which marks the head of the grave was brought from Connecticut and placed where it now stands.* We were told that the "Capin" John Brown,

---

* Beside the older is a newer grave containing the body of Watson Brown, brought here and laid near the father, October 12, 1882, after remaining unburied for nearly twenty-three years. Considered by the authorities of Virginia simply as that of a criminal, it was given after death to the Medical College at Winchester and there preserved as an anatomical specimen—the mother appealing in vain for the privilege of giving it Christian burial. Later, when the town was occupied by the Union forces, it was carried off by an Indiana surgeon and kept by him as a curiosity until in 1882, when he informed the survivors of its whereabouts and offered to restore it for more decent interment. From Indiana the poor, buffeted body went to the mother in Ohio, and was finally brought here and laid to rest beside the "big rock," where he had played as a boy while learning strange theories of "duty."

whose name heads the list, was the John Brown's father, in which case John must have been born an orphan as this one died something over twenty-three years before the young man was born. There must be some mistake about it somewhere, as even after careful inquiry of the people in charge, we could not find out that he ever had a father.

We passed up over the big rock bearing the inscription, cut in large letters, "John Brown, 1859," and to the house to learn something more concerning it.

"Don't you want to stay all night?" said the little girl, with an eye to business.

I glanced at the grave, the cold rock and the dreary, darkening fields around, and said "No." Then a boy member of the family cornered Att., and eloquently held up to him the advantages of seeing the "stun" by daylight! But Att. couldn't see it. Then the loquacious lady of the house met the Professor at the door with the continuation of what the boy and girl had started, but the Professor being a modest man threw the responsibility on me, and, alas! all I wanted was information.

"We can accommodate you if you want to stay," said she, bringing the register.

We said no again, counted, and found that over four hundred besides ourselves had registered during the summer.

"Got as good rooms as anybody, and everybody who has stopped here has been satisfied," continued she insinuatingly.

"Almost everybody buys these," said the little girl, producing a pair of stereographs of the grave and rock: "fifty cents for the two."

We meekly produced the plaster and inquired if they owned the place.

"No," said the mother, "We've only been here a little while, but take in strangers who want to stay all night and——"

"This is the house old John Brown used to occupy, isn't it?"

"Yes, but we've fitted it up new some since, and now you can't find no better rooms——"

"What has become of the widow and children?"

"I don't know just where, but out West somewhere, I believe. We just take care of it and keep folks who—"

"It seems to be all forest to the south; is there a path leading from here to the Indian Pass?"

"Yes. Parties often come through and stop overnight or get something to eat; and I don't like to say it myself, but they always seem satisfied with our fare. Now—"

"I am gathering information for a book on the Adirondacks, which is my reason for asking so many questions. Now if you have any interesting information concerning this locality I will be—"

"Well, now, I think if people knew that we were prepared to keep folks and was always prepared to get up meals, with game and trout always on hand, they would come more; and if you will just state—"

"All right; good evening, madam."

"We should like to—folks say they were just as well kept as at a hotel—might just mention trout—game dinners—venison nearly all the time—barn room— people — haven't — found — it — out — much — yet —it's—getting purty—dark—hadn't—you—better— stay?"

As we passed out of hearing the thought would come that if the old man could sleep there unmoved for a term of years, the angel Gabriel would have to be in pretty good lip to start him at the end of time.

We had aimed to stay at Lake Placid on the night of our visit to the grave of John Brown, but decided to stop at the North Elba Hotel, a very pretty little

72

two-story house, with wings extending out from the main part, accommodating about 25 guests. It is on the Post road, between Elizabethtown and Saranac Lake, 25 miles from the former—10 from the latter, and two miles from Lake Placid. Mr. Lyon, the proprietor, is one of those sturdy farmer-looking men who, besides being postmaster, justice of the peace and nobody knows what else, is considered to have a sort of fatherly interest in everything going on in the neighborhood. The literature displayed was of the most solid character: History, a Gazetteer, Congressional Proceedings, "with the compliments" of the lawmakers, etc. But we felt more like devouring the supper, which was like the literary food—substantial. Afterward we disappeared for the night.

Nash's, Mirror Lake

Brewster's Lake Placid House

Chapter VIII

Lake Placid—Bloomingdale—Paul Smith's—Martin's

In the morning, retracing our course of the night before for a few rods, we turned toward the north, and passing through a piece of woods nearly a mile in extent, came out upon the shores of Mirror Lake.

Mirror Lake is a pretty sheet of water about one mile in length by half that in width, and was known as "Bennett's Pond" until an enthusiastic young lady composed a lot of poetical stuff concerning it and gave it its present euphonious name. (There! that word has worried me. I have been trying for some time and am thankful that I have disposed of it at last very nicely. My attention was attracted to it at first by noticing that everyone who wrote about Lake George worked in "euphonious" in some way or other. I have more in reserve which I intend to precipitate on the reader at some future time.)

Nash's, near the north end of Mirror Lake, is well known and liked by sportsmen; J. V. Nash, the proprietor, is the oldest settler in the neighborhood.

The Lake Placid House, a little beyond Nash's, usually spoken of as "Brewster's," is a large, comfortable-looking house with broad piazza on two sides, standing on the ridge that separates Mirror Lake from Lake Placid.

Lake Placid is called by some the gem of the Adirondacks, but while it possesses many attractions, there are probably others equally fine. It is about five miles long and two broad, measuring through the islands, of which there are three, and which are so large that the lake resembles a large river sweeping around them rather than a lake with islands.

Since leaving Wilmington we had passed south nearly half way around Whiteface Mountain, and now looked at it from the southwest to where it seemed to rise directly up out of the lake, although in fact removed nearly two miles. A small pond near by attracts some attention, having the name of "Paradox Pond." It is connected with Lake Placid by its outlet, which is also its inlet, being each in turn, and through which it is said its waters ebb and flow like the ceaseless motion of the tide.

Saranac Lake in late 1870's

After dinner we succeeded in removing Att. from the presence of a fascinating divinity in calico, and started for Saranac Lake; then, as we neared that place

Bloomingdale in late 1870's

concluded to push on to Paul Smith's by way of
Bloomingdale. Bloomingdale has a very pretty
name, a very new-looking hotel, very few houses,
a very good-looking frame which was started for a
church and now stands, considerably darkened by
time, patiently waiting to be roofed and clap-
boarded. It was late in the afternoon when we left
Bloomingdale for Paul Smith's, and a rain threatening;
but Att. knew the way perfectly, because he told us
so, and it was only seven or eight or nine or ten miles
there. We started and on the way tried an old amuse-
ment of asking everybody we met the distance to our
place of destination. Almost invariably we got for reply the distance there from the home of the one
questioned. Thus we continued for some time to meet
persons who gave us the distance from Bloomingdale. It was interesting but hardly satisfactory, especially when night descended and the rain came down
on our umbrella-less heads, and trickled down
our necks and settled in the seat beneath us.

"Here's where we turn," said Att., wheeling around

77

to the left. Then he pulled up to inquire the distance of a man at the side of the road.

" 'Bout six miles if you turn round and go t'other way," said the man.

Att. turned around. He knew the way, of course—such a good joke! A little way farther we found that it was four miles to Smith's; then an individual reckoned it was about seven miles; then, as we failed to meet any one to inquire of, we had to thrust in Providence. We told stories the rest of the way while the rain patterned down on the leaves and on the muddy road in a contented sort of manner. It dripped from the branches of the trees and our hats and noses, and the horse got tired and wanted to walk all the way, and jokes wouldn't crack on account of the dampness.

William H. Smith, Bloomingdale hermit (Photo from Titus's Adirondack Pioneers)

But we were thankful when Att. knew all about the way! He was so comical and full of spirits. He gave every guidepost a critical examination, and the last one that we came to—at the forks of the road which led out into the dark woods—he got out, and hugged and kicked and grunted up to the shingle on top. After sacrificing sundry matches, with his eyes and fingers and great difficulty, succeeded in finding out that he couldn't tell anything about it; so he slid down, and in a drizzly, uncertain sort of way, got in, and we started again. Then we recollected the line of telegraph poles that ran along by the road and were jubilant, for we knew that by following it we would bring up at Paul Smith's. So we went by telegraph the rest of the way.

"This road isn't much traveled," said Att., as we plunged down a hill into what looked like a tunnel, through overhanging trees.

"Never mind; don't you see the telegraph?" we stuck to that as our last drop out of the harness, the wagon gave a lurch to one side and nearly lost its load, brought up and went the other way. After jerking about like a man with two wooden legs trying to get down a pair of stairs, it rested at the bottom of a gully which had been dug out by some freshet, and considered so bad that they had built a road around rather than repair it. Luckily our tired beast had taken the center. Att. was proud of her—"so kind and gentle." She was all of that, and more. For a persevering, go-ahead-and-ask-no-question sort of beast, I never saw her equal.

A little way farther we saw a dusky strip of water through a grove of tall pines and on the shore a large house. Lights gleamed and welcomed us onward, and soon we were seated around a crackling fire, with a room full of guides, dogs and sportsmen, who smoked and told stories until the clock struck twelve. Then we withdrew and went to sleep listening to the patter of the raindrops on the roof.

Paul Smith's Hotel

"Paul Smith's" is a surprise to everybody—an astonishing mixture of fish and fashion, pianos and puppies, Brussels carpeting and cowhide boots. It is surrounded by a dense forest.—Out of the way of all travel save that which is its own, it is still near the best hunting and fishing grounds. (For the matter of that, however, the hotels are all in the very best, if the veracious circulars can be relied on) A first-class watering-place hotel, with all the modern appliances, set right in the midst of a "howling wilderness." Around the house the timid deer roam. Within they rest. Without, the noble buck crashes through the tangled forest. Within, he straddles elegantly over the billiard tables and talks horse. On the lake theoretical veterans cast all manner of flies. In the parlors the contents of huge Saratoga trunks are scientifically played, and nets are spread for a different kind of fish. Poodles and pointers, hounds, setters, dandies and others of the species are found. Feathers and fishing rods, point lace and pint bottles are variously mixed. Embryo Nimrods—who never knew a more destructive weapon than a yard-stick—are seen hung all around with revolvers and game-bags and cartridge-pouches and sporting guns that are fearfully and wonderfully made. Here, you must know, danger is to be faced. Even the ladies *bare* arms, and at such times are very dangerous sportsmen indeed.

There are two St. Regis lakes—Upper and Lower. The upper lake is about 3½ miles long, the water passing through Spitfire Pond to the lower lake, and out through the St. Regis River to the St. Lawrence. The lower lake is about two miles long and one in width. The surrounding country is rather tame, lacking the high mountains which are found farther south.

Paul Smith came here in 1859, built a small house among the pines and commenced keeping sportsmen, in which he was very successful. At present he shows a large three-story hotel, with accommodations for over a hundred guests. There is also a large house for the use of guides, and a fine set of stables for his own and other horses that may come. It is thirty-seven miles to "Point of Rocks," the southern terminus of the Plattsburgh Railroad, to which place, during the season, a daily line of stages run. The telegraph, which

Paul Smith

Mrs. Paul (Lydia Martin) Smith

81

is carried into the house, places its occcupants within talking distance of the outer world, and speaks well for the enterprise of the proprietor.

In appearance Paul is not the man you would pick out as the one to keep a popular hotel. Rather above medium height, usually quiet, not appearing to have much to say about the house nor much to do but listen to stories and perform other like laborious duties usually expected of the keeper of a summer hotel.

The fond parents of the gentleman alluded to, when he was a youngster, broke away from the established custom of the rather extensive family to which they belonged and refused to name their offspring John. Instead they named him "Apollos A." His name was soon bobbed down to "Pol," then to "Paul" by those who were disgusted to find that "Pol" was only a man; and now, a letter directed to "Apollos A. Smith" would be very liable to be sent to the Dead Letter Office by the owner of the name himself. At all events "Paul Smith's" is a very popular resort, and patronized extensively by a wealthy class of visitors who prefer to rough it in a voluptuous sort of way.

Although it was rather late in the season when we were there, a few kindred spirits still lingered, who were personally and intimately acquainted with everybody from the Shah and Yankee Sullivan down to the Heathen Chinee and who, when night came, would gather around the stove in the office and to an appreciative audience of dogs, guides and themselves, review the drama, the arts and sciences, tell stories of fighting men and ministers, dogs and horses, hunting and fishing, interspersed with intensely interesting debates on the relative merits of plug and fine-cut. Also learned disquisitions on the proper position of the left auricle at that exciting moment when the fly has been cast, and a gamey two-ounce trout

82

has struck and hesitates as to the expediency of taking to the woods or the open field. On this much-vexed question authorities differ, and it is probable that it will always be a disputed point, as the physical development and temperament of the fish has to be taken into consideration. A fisherman as is a fisherman must be governed by circumstances. In fact, he must be a strategist of superior calibre, even like unto that of the most successful fisherman of whom we have any record who, after the fashion in those primitive days before they used flies as extensively as at present, swallowed a whale, and after a three days' struggle brought him safe to land. . . .

Sunday morning it rained. On account of the day the stories had a subdued spirit in them. The principal business was to get through with three meals and go to bed. Monday morning it rained. Dressed, ate breakfast, listened to stories; had supper, after which there were some stories told, interspersed here and there with stories, and occasionally a tale to give zest to the entertainment. Then more stories, and after another story or two we went to bed with a confused sort of an idea that a swarm of green and red and white and black and brown and yellow, and "scarlet ibis" and "green dragon flies," with lines tied to their heads and fish-hooks to their tails, sported playfully around our heads, floated enticingly near us, were scientifically cast or tantalizingly skittered across the water, tempting us to "rise." But we soon floated out into deep water and thus ended our last day at "Paul Smith's."

We had engaged a guide to go with us through the Saranacs to Long Lake, but when we opened our eyes on the morning of the 7th of October the ground was white with snow, and the trip had to be given up.

"By darn!" said the Professor, with an air of desperation, "I don't want to be snowed in up here in the woods all winter. Doesn't a stage leave here for somewhere?"

We found that one would go anywhere for a consideration. We engaged it to take us to Martin's at the north end of the lower Saranac, distant about fourteen miles by road and thirty by water—the route we had intended to take if the weather had been suitable.

How indescribably lovely the landscape appeared that morning. The great flakes danced and whirled and floated, crossing back and forth as if in play with each other as they fluttered downward through the air. They covered every stone, tree and shrub, clung to the delicate tamarack and hemlock, weighting down the sturdy spruce and pines until their branches bowed down gracefully beneath the load. Changed were the climbing vines into a delicate tracery of white; the long, wavy grasses and graceful ferns were frosted silver and the surrounding woods a grand, pure forest of pearl and milk-white glass. When we reached the open country new beauties came into sight. The fields stretched away in their dress of white, through which stone and stubble could be seen, softening and subduing the foreground, while fainter far away the hills rose up until lost in the falling clouds of beautiful snow.

Soon we became conscious that we had left the main road and were on one which required some little attention on our part to keep from doing injury to the interior of the stage. It was a good road—for a dyspeptic or one troubled with a poor appetite. The driver was apparently in something of a hurry. The ride cost us six dollars, but we got our money's worth. There was much variety to it. It was a good stage, too, and we, being the only occupants, had choice of position. We tried several. We braced ourselves up in the corners. We rattled around. We shot from side to

Kellogg and O'Brien stageline

side; made some good runs, caromed into each other and pocketed ourselves under the seats. We couldn't get knocked out, for the sides—excepting a lookout hole—were buttoned down and the roof firm. We were satisfied of that, for we tried it. Sometimes the Professor's side would rise up to get over a big stone, and he would start for me. I had striven with him repeatedly and remonstrated against such frequent and energetic calls and unceremonious visitations, but to no effect. Retribution was sure to follow, however, for when his side went down I would sail majestically over and light on him. That vehicle meandered playfully over stones and stumps and into holes. It would jump over logs when we, rising like young eagles, would soar away toward the roof. We like to soar, but to alight was the question. It would go down into deep holes and stop in such a decided sort of way that we would involuntarily feel our heads, expecting to find our backbones sticking up through our hats. When at last we reached Saranac Lake, it was with a feeling of "goneness" peculiar to those who have been without food for days and days.

Martin's, later Miller's, Saranac Lake House

Martin's is about the same distance from "Point-of-Rocks" as "Paul Smith's," viz: thirty-seven miles, and is considered the regular gateway to the Saranac and Tupper Lake regions. William F. Martin came here in 1849 and built a small house for the accommodation of sportsmen. He was among the first to attempt a sporting house in the wilderness. The house is on the shore of the lake at its northern extremity and provides for about two hundred guests. It is quite popular, although not as fashionable as "Paul Smith's," in the society sense of the word.

Chapter IX

Bartlett's—The Surly Clerk—The Fishball Encounter à la Murray

The morning after our arrival we started for the upper lake in one of Bartlett's freight boats, which chanced to be going up at that time. It was a lovely morning—a little frosty, but not uncomfortable—and the sun came out soon, clear and warm, raising delicate wisps of mist from the surface and making the snow-laden trees glitter with their millions of diamonds. Whiteface on the northeast and Marcy, with its surrounding peaks, away to the southeast—reflected in the glassy lake like great mountains of shining snow. The lower lake is six miles long, and said to contain an island for each week of the year. The shores are picturesque, at times rising in solid rock straight up, at others shelving smoothly out into the deep water.

At the southwest end of the lake, "in the shadow of a great rock," we entered a river fringed with flags and lilypads and tall, dead trees, marking what was once the shores, now covered with water—the effect of a dam which was built at the outlet of the lake, adding four feet to its original level and flooding back up this stream for something over a mile. A great many of the lakes and ponds of the wilderness have been dammed by the lumbermen and held in reserve for times when the volume of water in the beds of the rivers is not sufficient to carry the logs along; then the gates are hoisted and the flood goes down carrying everything before it. The result of this overflow of the natural boundaries of the lakes has been to kill the vegetation on the shores, and the beauty of many of them has been seriously impaired by this border of dead and dying trees. Something over a mile was passed when we came to the falls—but little more than rapids—where the water shoots down through a smooth, rocky channel with a swish and a curl or two at the bottom. We stepped ashore, and while one held the boat away from the rock the others pulled it up through the cut, then got aboard again and picked our way slowly up stream.

Guideboat and scow on Saranac River near Bartlett's

The ordinary Adirondack boat is a model of beauty, narrow and nearly alike at the ends. Above the water-line it is widened out somewhat——seldom enough, however, to allow a small boy to sit way back in the stern. This is well enough in a small boat, but the principle seemed grotesque enough when applied to one that would carry a ton. Our craft was of the stereotyped mould and dragged heavily, at times requiring the help of all to push and paddle her over the bars. We suggested that a part of the cargo be carried further forward to trim ship properly, but the captain —there was a captain and one crew—allowed that he had loaded a good many boats in his life and never had to shift the load either (actual measurement showed that we drew two inches of water forward and eighteen at the stern), and his position was triumphantly maintained until we dragged over the sandy bottom into Round Lake and up to "Bartlett's," followed by a series of swells such as follow in the wake of a propeller.

Round Lake is about two and one-half miles in diameter and, as its name implies, nearly round in shape. It contains several pretty rocky islands. The shores are bold and at the time were brilliant in their autumn dress. Passing across, we went out on the west side between two great rocks, and up a slow stream half a mile to "Bartlett's."

"Bartlett's" is at the foot of the short carry, between Round Lake and the Upper Saranac. Here the boats are taken from the water and transported to the upper lake on a cart at a cost of fifty cents for each boat. The house, which will accommodate about fifty, is a long, low, old-fashioned structure, with a rambling, uncertain look about it and its outbuildings, as though they were dropped down here and there as a temporary sort of arrangement. The interior is pleasant, containing some well-furnished rooms. The ta-

Bartlett's

ble is excellent. It is reached principally by the route we pursued and has no connection with the outer world save by boat or through the wild woods. The proprietor, Mr. Bartlett, has lived there for many years, and his host of friends will regret to learn that he is to give up the business.

"Yes," said he, "I've had enough of it. I've slaved as long as I am going to, and I'm going to sell out. Never'll take another boarder as long as I live, unless it's some old friend, like Dr. Ely, for instance." Bartlett is a short, thick-set man, with a brusque way of speaking that sounds cross until you catch the kindly twinkle in his eye. My numerous questions concerning his affairs seemed to bother him until I explained that, in a small way, I was connected with the press.

"The press!" said he, with a snap; "damn the press! I've been pressed to death. I don't want anything more to do with it; I don't care what they say about me." Then, with a twinkle in his eye, he told some things that the "press" had said of him, which showed him to be not entirely lost to its blandishments.

After dinner we decided to take a trip through the upper lake and return at night (as the course we had marked out simply led across the south end of it), and thought it would do no harm to put out a trolling line —possibly we might strike something—so we applied to the clerk for the necessary articles. All, or nearly all, of the sporting houses advertise to furnish fishing-tackle and everything required for the sport, but this clerk didn't appear particularly anxious to spring around and produce them. He was devoted to his duties behind a little counter that fenced off one corner of the room, and afforded retreat for sundry mysterious-looking bottles. Some folks would have taken it for a bar; but, bless you! it was no such thing. At least the only drinks called for were "opodeldo" and "laughing-gas," and everybody knows that neither of these articles is spirituous.

At last he said he would try to rig me up, so he started out. In the course of a half hour I found him sitting contentedly on the porch, where he had stopped to rest, and was soothed with the information that he didn't believe there was any use trying to troll. I thought so myself, but nevertheless as long as I had set out with that intention I proposed to continue, so he started again. After another lapse of valuable time I found him in the guide-house, serenely seated on a dry goods box, swinging his legs back and forth and drumming with his fingers in a dreary sort of way. I was grieved to interrupt his reverie, but it seemed necessary.

"Where's that line?" I asked.

"Hain't got none." Then he whistled a little tune.

"But don't you advertise to supply such things?"

The question didn't seem to interest him much, but he stopped whistling long enough to say, "Yes."

"Well! Can you do it?"

My perseverance in the insane desire seemed to

excite a mild surprise in his brain. He said Bartlett had had some that summer, but he guessed they were all lost—anyway he didn't know where they were. I don't blame the clerk. Not a bit. He was overworked. Nearly tired out at the time and did give out later so that he had to be put to bed quite early in the evening. At last, by aid of a guide, we succeeded in getting a line and started.

The Upper Saranac is about eight miles long and perhaps two wide, the longest way being north and south. It discharges toward the east from its south end through an arm which is nearly two miles deep, then making quite a rapid descent for the distance of a hundred rods to where, at its foot, is situated "Bartlett's"—our stopping place. It contains a number of rocky islands, some of them high and bold. The

Prospect House, later called Saranac Inn

92

shores are thickly wooded and picturesque, the country around quite level, but the hills round about can scarcely lay claim to the title of mountain. At its head is the Prospect House, a clean, white building with a thrifty look that speaks volumes in its favor.

We reached "Bartlett's" on the return soon after dark. I didn't get a bite, although I fished faithfully. Perhaps the velocity of our boat had something to do with our ill-luck, as the "gang" to which a shiner was attached would spring out of the water occasionally, and "skitter" along the surface like anything but a fish; but the spirit of Isaac Walton moved within me and I persevered. I had admired Murray for his wonderful skill, devoured the contents of "I go-a-fishing" with avidity and felt able to play anything, or throw any kind of a fly in existence. I felt the excitement of the veteran angler at the very sound of the word "fish." In imagination, with the great piscatorial lights of the age, my heart thrilled at sight of a pollywog and closed my eyes in an ecstasy of bliss as I thought of the terrific ravings of a half-ounce sucker fairly fast.

With such feelings surging through my breast we went in to supper. Ah! can it be possible? Yes, yes, it is! A school of fish-balls within easy reach! I will catch one! But what true fisherman can act the part of a butcher? True greatness in that line consists not in the amount creeled, but the manner of doing it. My heart thrilled with the excitement which the angler feels when the gently undulating motion of the atmosphere tells him that his quarry is nigh. I prepared for a cast. A moment's hesitation, in which the momentous question presented itself whether I had better take my "scarlet dragon" or "blue-tailed ibis." I tried both, but not a ripple stirred the quiet depths. Then I tried a spoon. Now I contend that it requires a great deal of skill to cast a spoon properly for a fish-ball, especially at this season of the year. Carefully I played it around over the bread; dragged it slowly across the potatoes, skittered it lightly over the butter and let it drop where I knew the wary creatures were lying in wait. Slowly it settled down, lightly as the dew into the heart of a blushing rose. A gentle ripple stirred the surface; I felt intuitively that the trying moment had come. A thrill shot up my arm and throughout my body to the very pit of my stomach as the beautiful creature curled upward and struck —struck hard! Then began the struggle—a struggle for life on the one side against science on the other. Mind against matter! It is an undoubted fact that an intellectual man, with a good spoon, is more than a match for any fish-ball that ever swam—and I proved it. Carefully I played him—for he was a gamey fish-ball. The surrounding gravy was lashed into fury— foaming white as the driven snow, but the cruel spoon held him as, with a sullen shaking he rested on the bottom—preparing for another run. Now he darts away like a flash of light, and is brought up by my gradually, though firmly compressing arm. Then he turned. He clove his native element as the thunderbolt a summer squash. The spoon brought him up once more and he turned directly toward us. It was a critical moment—a moment of terrible suspense!

"Give him the butt!" screamed the Professor, dodging behind the teapot; "give him the butt!"

"Stand firm, Professor!" I cried, controlling myself with great difficulty wrought up to the highest pitch of excitement as the enraged fish-ball sprang several feet in the air and made directly for me with my mouth open wide. "Stand firm, and the victory is ours."

I gave him the butt as he came, and the split bamboozine bent as a reed shaken in the wind! Oh! the terrific fire that blazed from the eye of that fish-ball will haunt me till my dying day. Rage, agony, despair, all blended in one as, shaking the sparkling drops of gravy from his gleaming sides he sprang entirely over us and plunged downward on the other side to again renew the attack. But I resisted. Suffice it to say that at the expiration of an exciting hour and sixty-nine minutes' sport, I succeeded in safely landing that heroic creature and laid him—a conquered fish-ball, at my feet. Science had triumphed.

Mr. Murray says, that "the highest bodily beatitude he ever expects to reach, is to sit in a boat with John at the paddle, and match again a Conroy rod against

Mother Johnson and her home at Raquette Falls between Upper Saranac and Long Lake — (drawing by Stoddard)

a three-pound trout;" but as for me, give me my trusty spoon, or even sharp stick. I care not who sits at the paddle, and let me once more feel the deathless joy of a single-handed encounter with an untamed fish-ball, and I'll murmur not even though a yawning legislature opens and sucks me in forever. Gentle reader, pardon this ebullition. I can never keep cool when so excited. Right here I must lift my voice against the horrible practice of coarse natures whose soul never swept upward to a spiritual conception of flies, who, with no excuse, save perhaps that of hunger, can, with a common hook and line, and filthy worms for bait, snatch a kingly trout baldheaded, and lay him gasping in uncomfortable terror on the ground. I cannot find words of condemnation strong enough to express my horror of this barbarous practice, which is extremely vulgar, contributes nothing to science, and is in all probability excessively annoying to the fish.

On the contrary, the scientific allurement of a denizen of the aqueous fluid to one more volatile is an achievement worthy of a great intellect. The skillful playing prepares the noble creature for its final transition which, if not actually attended with pleasurable sensations to the subject in question, must be owing to its lack of appreciation of the important part it is playing in the march of intellect. It is also more Christian-like and refined than bull baiting, because less dangerous, and we cannot wonder that great minds are sometimes translated by its wonderful fascinations.

Chapter X

Long Lake—Guides and Carries

Long Lake is about fourteen miles in length and one in width at the widest, which is near its outlet. It receives the waters of the Raquette River at its head, and gives them up to the same name at its foot. Thence, the water flowing northward, and passing within three miles of the Saranacs, turns towards the southwest, touching the foot of Big Tupper's Lake, then northwesterly past Potsdam to the St. Lawrence. Long Lake contains several islands. Round Island,

Island House, Long Lake

nearly midway between the inlet and outlet, resembles Dome Island of Lake George, but is more perfect in its dome-like appearance. Near the head of the lake, on the west, is the Owl's Head, a mountain marked on the map as 2,706 feet above tide, but as Long Lake is 1,575 feet above the ocean, the Owl's Head isn't much of a mountain after all. To the west the country is level. On the east is Mount Kempshall, originally called Long Mountain. On the north is seen the blue serrated summit of Mount Seward, 5,000 feet above tide.

Here, at Long Lake, the road from Pottersville and Schroon touches, thence turning south, continues along the east shore and southwest, past Raquette Lake, at places being little more than a mere trail and known as the Carthage road. The land around, while apparently promising well, is cold and ill-adapted to farming purposes. Some of the clearings were made upwards of forty years ago and quite good buildings put up, but a blight seems to have come over them. The township contains about 300 inhabitants, who subsist principally by guiding through the summer, and hunting and trapping in the winter.

Mitchell Sabattis, a noted Indian guide, who has figured extensively in all histories of that region, deserves more than a passing notice. He was born at Parishville, St. Lawrence county, September 29, 1801. A pure-blood of the tribe of St. Francis, he early took to the woods as naturally as a duck to water. On the death of his mother, which occurred when he was but seven years of age, his father, "Captain Peter," as he was universally called, used to take young Mitchell along on his various hunting and trapping expeditions. The Captain, who earned his right to the title by his service in that capacity during the war of the Revolution, is said to have been a noble speci-

Mitchell Sabattis, famed hunter and guide

men of a man—mentally as well as physically, and lived to the advanced age of 108. As a proof of his physical powers a place is still pointed out a little below Raquette Pond, known as "Captain Peter's rock," from which he once leaped to the shore, fully sixteen feet distant.

Mitchell is earnest, intelligent and thrifty, a member of the Methodist church, is authority for many things relating to Indian history, has probably seen more of wood life than any other man in the wilderness. He is a fearless and successful hunter and is admitted by the other guides to have the best knowledge of the woods of any man in the country. He killed his first deer when thirteen years of age, and since then the number that have fallen before his unerring rifle is legion. He has also killed several bears and nine panthers. He drove one of the latter along a narrow shelf on the face of a ledge, into a crevice, from which he was dislodged by two or three vigorous punches with a sharp stick in order that a companion might get a shot at him; but when, for some unaccountable reason the man failed, Sabattis himself dispatched the beast. In his earlier days moose were plenty in the woods and Sabattis has killed twenty of these huge animals, the last being in 1854. The old hunter is still hale and hearty, bidding fair, with his iron constitution, to guide for many years to come.

Long Lake Village, commonly called "Gougeville," is situated on the east side of the lake, three and one-half miles from its head. It is composed of eighteen to twenty buildings, assorted sizes, a school house, church, store, post office, and what is of more interest to the average traveler, Kellogg's popular hotel. At present I have no vivid recollection of a "Sabbath in the woods," but in this connection do remember one spent in "Gougeville" three or four years ago, which was ushered in by a general brightening up of guns and sorting of fishing-tackle that indicated anything but a devotional spirit as the word is generally understood; and it seemed to show that there was a variety of opinion as to the proper manner of celebrating the day in question. On that occasion I concluded to attend divine worship and in due time found myself seated in the little church listening to an earnest discourse from the minister who was also blacksmith, lawyer, shoemaker and merchant in a small way, besides devoting his leisure hours to meditation and farming. The interior of the church was not what could properly be styled luxurious, but it was substantial.

Over the pulpit, and occupying a considerable portion of that end of the building, was an immense marine clock, great in the display of gold, while letters on its face explained that it was "presented by Dr. Todd's Mission S. School," from somewhere or other—I don't remember where just now. But I understand that the philanthropic donors are at present engaged in a laudable endeavor to furnish overcoats to the suffering Hottentots. It did seem like discouraging work for a frail mortal of a minister-man to attempt to lead minds away on the ocean of eternity with time staring them so squarely in the face. Uneducated as we were in the science of mellifluous strains, we could but notice the vast difference between the rendition of familiar pieces by the choir, and the high-spiced oleo of sacred song dispensed by the $20,000 kind. There was no sinful mixing of "Old Hundred" with the latest operas; no voluptuous waltzes trickling down through tortured "Coronation;" no basso profundo howling in "Le Diable"—revamped for Sunday ears; no fancy runs, artistic slides or coltish whinnying in the upper register, but primitive purity undefiled ruled the hour. The leader lead off gallantly, and as soon as it became known what tune he had started a female voice dashed in and made great exertions to close up the gap between. Then voice after voice took up the strain that rose and swelled until it seemed that three or four blended together like half a dozen. Some wandered away and foundered. The high soprano made several gallant dashes to pass the leader, but he kept to his knitting and came out first—winning the heat by a good half-length, while the bass "Came rumbling after."

Three or four years ago someone put a few pickerel into Long Lake to see if they would breed. They did. They multiplied and replenished the pickerel world in a way truly wonderful. Now it is rare sport for amateur sportsmen, but the guides want to get hold of the man who put the first pickerel in. They do not fancy the slime which goes with the fish, which they call a hog, ready to bite anything that comes

101

along from a dishrag to a small boy.

Long Lake has one industry wherein it stands at the head, that of boat-building. A "Long Lake boat" in the Adirondacks is considered the synonym of all that is graceful and perfect in that line. The regulation boat is about 3 feet wide, from 14 to 17 long, weighing when new, from 60 to 80 pounds, and costing about one dollar per pound.

We sent our Saranac guide back and inquired for one who understood the Raquette region.

"I know the man you want," said our host in a way as though he felt himself responsible for our future happiness; "Charles Blanchard knows all about it— just came from that region day before yesterday. I'll send for him."

He did so, and soon a little fellow in a Garibaldian shirt stood before us. Thinking of the work a guide is supposed to do, it seemed as though this one was meant for a joke or an ornamental head that we would have to carry over the rough places. Kellogg must have noticed the look of surprise on our faces for, taking me aside, he said:

"Oh, he's all right: knows the country better'n I do my house, and he will take you right every time."

"Carry a boat, too?" I asked incredulously gazing at the slight figure.

"Yes, sir! Carried a boat, oars and all, over the same route a day or two ago. Then he can learn you something—tell you all you want to know. There's no need of his guiding at all only he likes it. I tell you what, sir, he's qualified for better things. He's—a—Schoolmaster!!"

We were overwhelmed and engaged the Schoolmaster, a pleasant companion and an exceptionally good guide, thoroughly acquainted with the region we were travelling through. Four miles from "Kellogg's" we came to the rapids. Here the Professor and myself took the loose articles, while the Schoolmaster started off with the inverted boat over his head, his shoulders fitting into the wooden yoke, on the ends of which the wales rested, and looking like a huge pickle dish on a pair of sinewy legs, slipping, but springing back and right-side-up every time. A half-mile carry brought us to still water, then a short distance of boating to Buttermilk Falls.

Reader, did you ever assist over one of these portages through the dense forest, where the path never dries and the decayed leaves and vegetable mould seems without bottom, a river of black muck with roots and stones projecting above the surface, which same are stepping places for the skillful but fearful traps for the unwary?

The guide takes the boat and you are expected to carry the lighter articles. You admire him as he starts out so lightly, stepping from rock to rock along the slippery path. Your soul swells with conscious freedom and you snuff in inspiration and black flies by the mouthful. You gather up oars, paddles, guns, fish-rods, etc., and step out determined to show that you too are a natural woodsman. How exhilarating the action of spreading from rock to rock, incidentally watching your feet that they do not get the start of you. The solid bottom may be anywhere from two inches to two feet below the surface, and the bushes scratch your hands and slap you in the face without the slightest provocation. After a while you find that the oars and other things are on a tender place, and you change only to make it worse. They also have a disagreeable habit of spreading out at various angles to straddle saplings, going on one side of trees which you had designed to pass on the other. You back up for another start, wrench your neck and get a crick in your back in the struggle to dodge the various limbs that are making unprovoked lunges at you, and at last your foot glides gently down and disappears in the inky depths.

Surprise, perspiration and determination appear on your face. Matters are getting interesting, and you careless of results. The guide is disappearing through the trees, the things on your shoulders are more sprawly than ever; the saplings crowd closer to the path. Then one or other side catches an oar, and they shut up on your aching neck like a pair of shears; a friendly limb lifts your hat and drops it in the mud right where you were going to step, so as to save your hat you make some playful passes in various ways, one foot gets on top of the other, then they wander off in different directions and you sit down. The chances are that about this juncture you begin to talk to yourself. It depends something on how you were brought up.

It is a delightful sensation to sit down—in the wild woods—after violent exercise—and rest. Gentle zephyrs steal refreshingly across your brow, back and insinuatingly into your clothes. At such a moment as this, free from the thraldom of civilization, in the solemn stillness of the mighty forests, with a soul attuned to the inspiring harmony of nature, your thoughts wander back to childhood's happy hours, and in the ecstasy of the moment some well-remembered passage learned at Sabbath-school comes welling up from your joyous heart. Bible quotations are liable to get somewhat mixed, however, and a disinterested beholder is likely to misconstrue your devotional expression. The most a man wants at such an hour is undemonstrative sympathy.

Chapter XI

Raquette Lake—Alvah Dunning
—Ned Buntline—Blue Mountain Lake

A half-mile carry brought us to still water, then a short distance of boating to Buttermilk Falls (which also lays claim to being Murray's "Phantom Falls!") Here the water dashes and foams down over the rocks, making a descent of about twenty-five feet, and the name, though not very poetical, was probably suggested by the churning that it gets in reaching the bottom.

Buttermilk Falls near Long Lake

"Murray's talk about shooting the falls in his boat in pursuit of the phantom form is a very probable story for a minister to tell," said the Schoolmaster with a contemptuous shrug. "It would sound better for one of us guides, though. Why, I drove a brood of ducks down over there once; the old one knew better than to go—she flew upstream—but they—a dozen of the young ones—went over, and only three came out alive. *He* talked of doing it! There isn't Baptist enough about him, but there's one thing he can 'shoot,' that's the long bow."

Alas for Mr. Murray's reputation for veracity, the beautiful creations of his fancy, the bright pictures conjured up by his fertile brain, are held as witnesses against him, simply because he, in his lavish generosity, enriched the common occurrences of every-day life in the woods with the precious incense of conceptive genius, leaving a dazzled world to separate the real from the ideal! The guides take him literally and have come to the conclusion generally that if his preaching is not a better guide to heaven than his book to the Adirondacks, his congregation might manage to worry along with a cheaper man.

We put the boat in the quiet water above and went upward a mile and a half, then over a portage of the same distance, which brought us to Forked Lake.

Forked Lake is about five miles in length, and appropriately named, as it is nearly all forks, a confusing train of alternate points and bays on the north, although on the south the shore is comparatively straight. We passed the outlet of Raquette Lake and soon landed on the south shore at an old clearing, four miles from where we came in, where stood the blackened ruins of what was once a sporting house. Then through a half mile of cleared ground now overgrown with bushes, down into the tall timberland across the Carthage road, and we stood on the shores of Raquette Lake.

Raquette Lake, the "Queen Lake of the Adirondacks," is indeed a lovely sheet of water, lacking only the grand old mountains to make it all that heart could wish; it is over 1,700 feet above tide, surrounded by trees of almost every variety to be found in the wilderness, which stretches away in gentle undulations on all sides, with here and there a mountain ridge or peak rising above its fellows.

Where we first stood on the shore, the sombre pines lined the water's edge and extended downward in inky shadow. Toward the west the portals widened out in successive shady coves, and bold rocky promontories, fringed with crimson maples, green and golden beeches, and the silver birch. Through these gateways appeared gently sloping hillsides, edged with glittering sand that seemed to tremble in ecstasy under the heat waves of an unclouded sun.

Our course was westerly for a distance, then as we rounded a rocky promontory on the left and turned toward the south, a scene unparalleled for sweet, quiet beauty, burst on our enraptured sight. Behind us, across the glassy lake, a single boat was moving, leaving a double line of beaded silver to mark its course. Beyond, from the north shore, a point came out, its surface almost as level as the motionless lake itself; edged with a smooth white beach, covered with grand old forest trees that ran up clear and straight for many feet, while upward through them curled the faint blue smoke of some hunter's campfire. Now the shore sweeps around away to the west and comes back in the broad meadow and woodland of Indian Point, where once stood a village that has passed away, leaving only its name as the heritage of the red man. Then westward deep into Eagle Bay, and away toward the south, it approaches and recedes in alternate wooded capes and deep bays to meet others on the east where the low ridges come down to the lake side. Between them the silvery water reflects island gems and vistas of tender purple distance.

The day, like the two preceding and the one to follow, was indescribably lovely. Not a breath stirred the surface, nothing, save the Indian Summer haze, which itself seemed luminous, dimmed the splendor of the sun's beams. The shore seemed to pass by us, a panorama of beauty—a constantly changing flash of gorgeous colors, sombre shade, gleaming sand, and a glittering edge of light that marked the line between the real and the reflected.

"Who would hesitate for a moment between the dusty city and a life among the grand old forests and lakes?" asked the Schoolmaster. "How beautiful this free temple, where every thought is an anthem of praise and thanksgiving."

"Dem foin!" said the Professor from the bottom of the boat, opening one eye a little way; "Have you got such a thing as a sunshade or an umbrella about you?"

We spared him on account of his youth, but the Schoolmaster was sad. All his sentiment was crushed out of him. When we asked who made the clearings around the border of the lake, of which we saw three or four with rude log houses built thereon, he said: "I don't know; some darn fool, I suppose, who expected to make a fortune here farming, forty miles from nowhere." They are all deserted now.

Raquette Lake has nowhere an uninterrupted water line of more than eight or nine miles, but from its outlet to Indian Point, then south through what appears to be a great irregular mass of bays and points, hanging to that side of the lake proper, to its head, is about twelve, but so irregular and winding its edges, that it is estimated to have a shore-line of from 90 to 100 miles in extent. It contains a number of islands.

108

The largest, known as "Beach's," with an area of nearly 300 acres, is at the south end, covered principally with beech and maple, clean and clear almost as any park, affording a delightful camping place for those so disposed. Another favorite, although one can hardly go amiss in selecting a camping place here, is now known as "Murray's Island," so named in honor of the reverend sportsman who usually pitches his summer tent here. The original and appropriate name was "Osprey Island," from a species of large bird which built their nests and reared young year after year in the great pines that stand there.

Alvah Dunning's camp on Raquette Lake

At the foot of one of these giants old Alvah Dunning has built a bark shanty, and with his dogs lives there—a modern Robinson Crusoe. Two or three dogs came out with their master to see us. I cannot say welcome, for the dogs growled, and the old hunter growled, and our suddenly conceived idea of stopping there until the next day was changed by his surly permission when our desire was made known. So we continued on toward the east inlet.

Alvah Dunning, Adirondack guide

Old Alvah was in his normal condition—suffering from ill treatment. He has always been a sufferer, because he doesn't always look at things in the same light as others, and he believes to this day that it was only by chance, aided somewhat by an overruling Providence, that his life is spared, for did not "Ned Buntline," the terrible, chase him all over Blue Mountain Lake with intent to deposit lead in his venerable cuticle? It is said that he hunted for Ned one summer and a misunderstanding arose, to settle which, Alvah felt called upon to embezzle a boat of the novelist's, and after perforating it in various places to sink it in the lake. This manner of procedure struck Ned as being out of order, so as a preliminary move he shot the old man's dog one day, while the latter was standing between his master's legs. Alvah was grieved thereby, and with a longing to indulge in cremation, threatened to set the "Eagle's Nest" on fire. When asked about the affair, Ned said, "I drove him out of that section when I was there because he threatened my life. The Old Rip steered clear of me after he found that I was as ready to throw lead as he was threats."

It is said that the first house at Raquette Lake was built on Indian Point, then one nearly opposite by a Mr. Wood, who lived there about twenty years, then became discouraged and left. Now the sole occupant of this fair land is old Alvah Dunning, the hermit of the Raquette.

Marion River, often called the East Inlet, is the largest feeder of the Raquette. Toward this we turned the bow of our boat, and soon the quiet stream received us, shutting us in from the golden, queenly lake. Away to the east between the low hills that rise gently from the marsh on either side, Blue Mountain seemed to beckon us on. Here the river is perhaps four or five rods in width, with an almost imperceptible current, hardly moving the lily pads that parted as our skiff scratched through the clusters, then drifted slowly back to their former position. This is a fair representative of a great many of the high country streams; deep, dark, still, covered with lily pads and bordered with a broad belt of reedy marsh. It is famed as a place for "floating," or jack-hunting, and we saw places where the ground was trodden by the hoofs of deer like that of a crowded sheepfold. For five miles the river was quiet, winding about so that, as the Professor suggested, "it would worry eels to follow;" then for another it rippled over sand and stones, where the overhanging alders slapped us in the face. Then followed a portage of a half-mile—two and a half more of boating across Utowana Lake, a half-mile or more through the dark woods with the yellow sunset sky at our backs for a guide. The pedagogue took the boat up through the shallow brook into Eagle Lake and around to where we waited. Then in the darkness we passed across to where a light shone out, and groping up the uneven slope found welcome and rest in the "Eagle's Nest," once the wilderness home of "Ned Buntline."

"Where the silvery gleam of the rushing stream
Is so brightly seen on the rocks dark green,
Where the white pink grows by the wild red rose
And the blue bird sings till the welkin rings.

"Where the red deer leaps and the panther creeps,
And the eagles scream over cliff and streams,
Where the lilies bow their heads of snow,
And the hemlocks tall throw a shade o'er all.

Where the rolling surf laves the emerald turf,
Where the trout leaps high at the hovering fly,
Where the sportive fawn crops the soft green lawn
And the crow's shrill cry bodes a tempest nigh—
    There is my home—my wildwood home."

"Ned Buntline," author of the above sweet lines that seem to rise upward like the joyous song of a wild bird, bringing thoughts of wild violets and the fragrance of dewy forests in its train. This strange man, with the blended nature of the tiger and the lark— the tender imaginings of a young girl and the uncontrolled passions of a wild beast—came here in 1856. He hoped to escape the dangers of civilization, and here had his alternate fierce battles and loving make-ups with his greatest enemy—the bottle. He

112

gave the place and the lakes around the names they now bear and lived here at odd times until the war cloud broke out over the South, when his restless, venturesome nature called him to the field. Out of the war he came unscathed, but the end is not yet. Whether it will be up through clearer paths to light, or downward with his lifelong foe, cannot be foretold, while the great curse is left to blacken the land.

Ned Buntline (Edward Zane Carroll Judson)

"Ned Buntline" (Edward Z.C. Judson) was born at Stamford, N.Y., March 20, 1823. His adventurous career began in early childhood. He killed his first deer when eight years of age, ran off to sea at eleven, was promoted to midshipman when only thirteen, the same year fought seven duels with fellow-midshipmen who refused to mess with him on account of his supposed inferiority, and threatened to deplete the whole budding navy unless he was acknowledged as an equal. The navy wilted! He served with credit in the Seminole war, and in the Mexican war, and when the war cloud broke over the South, his venturesome spirit called him to the field once more. Five wounds by sabre and bullet, one of which made him lame for life, testify to his service for the country he served so proudly and gladly, while with fine scorn he refused the proffered pension. Later, at intervals, as novelist, dramatist, actor and temperance advocate he filled the public mind like—no one under the sun but only "Ned Buntline," the irrepressible. His first story, "The Captain's Pig," was published in his fifteenth year. As a writer of "Frontier Fiction" he was unexcelled. Buffalo Bill, Texas Jack, and Wild Bill were made famous by his stories of border life. His income as a story writer amounted to $20,000 annually. His literary productions would make more than two hundred large volumes.

But the old eagle has flown, other birds of prey occupy the nest. A brood of young ones gathered around, climbed on us, counted our buttons, pulled our hair, and made us generally welcome, and the way we went for the food set before us would have made ordinary birds of prey tremble for their reputation. This, the only house in the locality, affords a comfortable stopping place for sportsmen through the summer months, and for lumbermen during the winter. A gang of these hardy sons of toil came in while we were there, took their supper, and when we thought they were fairly settled for the night and were apparently going off in a nice snooze, those men of Belial got up, knocked around the furniture and stove, rattled pots and kettles until the rooms were full of steam and the air of frizzled pork and profanity. Then away to the woods, whence with the first gray streaks of morning light, came the sound of their axes and the crash of falling trees.

When river-driving commences these men often stand all day long soaked with ice-cold waters that come down from the melting snows above. Only constitutions of iron can endure what they do at times, but as a class they are careful not to tax their strength by any needless intellectual pursuits, such as poring over newspapers or books in the glare of unhealthy lamps or anything of the kind. By their abstemious habits in these respects, many are enabled to earn from two to three dollars per day through the season, and endure it for eight or ten years before they become too stiff to move.

Eagle Lake is the middle link of the Eckford Chain, very pretty and about one mile long. At its east end the boat is pushed or towed up through a narrow channel from which the stones have been removed. Here the road from North Creek, thirty miles distant, crosses; parties sometimes entering the wilderness from this direction. But the condition of the road for half the distance is such that it is not very popular at present.

Blue Mountain Lake, or Lake Emmons, is called the gem of the smaller lakes. It is three miles in length, very irregular, especially along the west shore, and contains a number of picturesque islands, some of them mere rocks rising above the surface. It is also sometimes called Tallow Lake, because of an old Indian who mourned a canoe load of venison tallow with which he once started for the distant settlement. Alas! the wind blew, the treacherous waves engulfed it, and the noble Greasian paid deer for his temerity. On the east rises Mount Emmons, commonly called Blue Mountain, from the color which is popularly supposed to pervade it, and enters into nearly every picture of this region.

We had reached this, the head waters of the Raquette, and rested on the west beach, thirty-five miles as we had come and only five miles from where we left Long Lake, but between it and us was a mountain carry of three miles, not generally liked by the guides. The Schoolmaster decided the question of which route to take back by shouldering his boat and starting up over the mountain. The path was very good—a gradual ascent for some ways, then a long reach of swamp and open meadow land where the springy surface of matted grass and interlaced roots shook and bent over unknown depths of black muck that oozed up along the slippery stepping places and mingled with the snow of the week before which still remained. Then we descended the north side of the mountain into the forest-embowered waters of South Pond. A row of one and one-half miles carried us past the comfortable looking shanty of A. F. Tait to the outlet. Then came a portage of another mile to Long Lake, and by boat to "Kellogg's," where we astonished the proprietor by the earnest manner in which we devoted ourselves to business at the dinner table.

After dinner we chartered a seat in a farmer's wagon and went to "Aunt Polly's" at Newcomb to spend the Sabbath with its genial proprietor, John Davis.

Chapter XII

Cheney and the Deserted Village
of Adirondac

Thus far our travels had been principally by carriage of some kind or by boat. We had been almost around the great peaks but not among them. The mountains that now looked down on us from the north we had viewed from the other side. We had passed around to the west along up Long Lake; made a loop of over 40 miles in the trip to Blue Mountain and back, then east to Newcomb; now, we must trust to our feet to carry us over the route laid down. Thanks to the pure air, and our previous struggles over the various carries, we felt equal to the task, so on Monday morning, with knapsacks strapped on our backs, we started for Adirondac, the ruined village among the mountains, eighteen miles distant.

Soon we saw an old friend, the Hudson River, on whose bosom floated the wealth of nations, here so narrow that in places we could almost jump across it. From the north it came, moving sluggishly along between the dark balsams that lined its banks and extended, an apparently unbroken forest, for miles back, while away over beyond rested the faint blue crest of Tahawus, "the cloud-splitter." Six miles from "Aunt Polly's," the road divides, the south branch going to Minerva, and the other to the Lower Works, two miles distant, thence east to Root's hotel, 23 miles further.

"Tahawus," so called on the maps and in the postal department, is generally spoken of here as the Lower Works, to distinguish it from the upper Adirondack village. Once there were extensive buildings at this place. A long dam across the Hudson, here called the North River, once flooded the valley back to the outlet of Lake Sanford and heavy barges floated between carrying provisions up and bringing ore down. Now the dam gone, the old kilns are in ruins, dead trees mark the flat where the waters once stood, and there is, I think, but one family there, excepting those occupying the hotel which is a large white house with comfortable accommodations for 20 guests. But aside from its interest as a hotel is the fact that this is the home of John Cheney, "the mighty hunter" of the Adirondacks.

We stopped for dinner, partially to see the old man, and partially because we felt a peculiar sensation stealing over us—an indescribable something that had attacked us regularly three times a day of late. In answer to our summons, a young man appeared in the doorway, of whom we asked if we could have dinner.

"I dunno," said he.

After a suitable time given to silence, the subject was again advanced in the way of an assertion.

"W-e w-o-u-l-d l-i-k-e s-o-m-e dinner!"

The smile spread over the young man's face and increased in sickly strength. It was evident that he sympathized with us. Sympathy is good but won't sustain life. We made another effort:

"CAN we have dinner?"

He laughed a little, said "fifty cents," then laughed a little more and rested at a half smile ready to go off at the slightest provocation. I looked at the Professor and did not wonder that the young man had misgivings as to his intentions. The Professor looked at me and intimated that he was not surprised that the pleasant youth was in doubt as to mine. Time had passed lightly over our heads without improving our clothing in the least. I tried another tack:

"Is Mr. Cheney in?"

"Guess not, hah."

"Where is he?"

"Gone huntin', guess."

"Mrs. Cheney?"

A flickering smile seemed to admit that that fact could no longer be concealed.

"We would like to see her."

"Fifty cents—dinner—hah."

"But I want to see Mrs. Cheney."

"Can—spose—hah."

With a withering look at the Professor whose dilapidated appearance had undoubtedly brought us into such a plight, I started on a tour of discovery and found Mrs. Cheney flying around, preparing a dinner for us. Having evidently seen us coming she had concluded by our looks, that we needed something—which we soon had, and while enjoying it, she, in a pleasant, cheery sort of way, talked about her absent husband.

He was born in New Hampshire, June 26, 1800, living there and at Ticonderoga until 30 years of age. Finding that game was growing scarce, he shouldered his rifle, and calling his faithful dog, set out for the then almost unknown wilderness. For years he lived alone on what his gun brought him, and ever since, his life has been that of a hunter. Many stories are told indicating his coolness in times of danger, and his skill and daring as a hunter. An account of his

John Cheney, great hunter-guide
(Stoddard drawing)

perilous adventures would fill a large volume. Headley, the historian, saw him when he first visited this region thirty years ago, and speaks of him as having "none of the roughness of the hunter, but as one of the mildest, most unassuming, pleasant men to be met with anywhere." Mrs. Cheney said he had gone hunting with some of "the boys," "for," she continued, with a flash of pride in her sense of ownership, "if he is 73 years old, he can run in the woods now and beat most any of 'em when he feels like it. If you could see him and he happens to feel all right, you could find out a good deal, but he's awful changeable, either awful good or awful bad." We did not see him, but in reply to a letter, received the following in a firm readable hand:
* * * "I've always had a great love for the woods and a hunter's life ever since I could carry a gun, and have had a great many narrow escapes from being torn to pieces by bears, panthers, wolves and moose, and many a time I have had to put a tree between myself and an enraged bull moose. After a while,

120

finding a rifle unhandy to carry, I had a pistol made expressly for my use. The stock was made out of a birch root, the barrel was eleven inches long and carried a half-ounce ball, and is now on exhibition at the Geological rooms at Albany. I received one hundred dollars for it after it was pretty nearly worn out.

Once I was rowing after a large buck deer, when it was accidently discharged, the ball striking me about halfway between my knee and ankle. It came out on the other side just below my ankle joint, but being 14 miles from any habitation and alone, I only stopped long enough to see what harm it had done. Then seized my oars and started for him again as the thought struck me, that I may need that deer now more than ever. I caught up with him and made short work of it, took him ashore, dressed and hung him up, but I soon perceived that if I ever got out of the woods I must lose no time, as my boot was full of blood and my ankle began to pain me very bad. So I cut two crotched sticks, and by their help managed to get out of the woods, but it took me about eight hours; I only stopped to set down once, as it was so hard to start again.

"I could tell you lots of my adventures if I could see you, but find I must stop writing as it would take all the paper in the house to write one quarter of them."

Accompanying this was a photograph of the old hunter—a venerable looking face set in a framework of silvery hair and beard, bearing a kindly look over all, even though the eyes had a severe expression.

From the Lower to the Upper works it is ten miles over a passable road running north along the west side of the valley. Halfway up, the foot of Lake Sanford is reached, where boats can be taken if desired, although the best way, if not desirous of fishing, is to continue along the road. The lake is four miles long, the shores low and marshy, looking more like a broad river than a lake, as it rests between the hills on the west, and North River mountain on the east.

Just above the head of Lake Sanford is the "new forge," the huge building itself in a dilapidated condition, but the great stone furnace, forty feet square at its base, stands firm and solid as when made. A few rods beyond this is the ruined village, where a scene of utter desolation met our view.

Deserted village of Adirondac (Tahawus) — (Stoddard drawing)

Nearly a quarter of a century has passed away since the busy hum of industry sounded here. Where once was heard the crash of machinery and the joyous shouts of children at play is now the shrill bark of the fox or the whir of the startled partridge. In place of the music of voices, all was silence, solemn and ghostly. Over the mountains and the middle ground hung a dark funeral pall of cloud across which the setting sun cast bars of ashen light. They fell on the nearer buildings bringing out their unseemly scars in ghastly relief and lay in strips across the grass-grown street which led away into the shadow. On either side once stood neat cottages and pleasant homes, now stained and blackened by time. Broken windows, doors unhinged, falling roofs, rotting sills and crumbling foundations, pointed to the ruin that must surely come. At the head of the street was the old furnace, a part of one chimney still standing, another, shattered by the thunderbolt, lay in ruins at its feet. The waterwheel—emblem of departed power—lay motionless, save as piece by piece it fell away. Huge blocks of iron, piles of rusty ore, charcoal bursting from the crumbling kilns, great shafts broken and bent, rotting timbers, stones and rubbish lay in one common grave, over which living nature had thrown a shroud of creeping vines.

Near the center of the village was a large house said at one time to have accommodated one hundred boarders, now grim and silent. Near-by at the left stood the pretty school house. The steps, worn by many little feet, had rotted and fallen, the windows were almost paneless, the walls cracked and rent asunder where the foundation had dropped away, and the doors yawned wide, seeming to say not "welcome" but "go."

> "O'er all there hung a shadow and a fear,
> A sense of mystery the spirit daunted
> And said as plain as whisper in the ear,
>   The place is haunted."

As we advanced a dog appeared at the side of the house and howled dismally; then, as if frightened at the sound of its own voice, slunk away again out of sight. We knocked at the door, but no sound save a hollow echo greeted us from within; that was

123

also deserted. Then we went out in the middle of the street where, suspended in a tree, hung the bell that used to call the men to work, and on the Sabbath, perhaps the villagers to worship in the little schoolhouse near by. Clear and sweet, pure and fearless, its tones rang out over the forests, away to the mountains, then back to us dying out in soft echoes. With it went the cloud that had oppressed our spirits.

Once more we knocked at the door of the large house, invited ourselves to enter and, passing through the sounding hall, made our way to the back portion of the house, which bore signs of having been recently occupied, foraged around until we discovered that there was no danger of immediate starvation, then built up a fire and set about preparing our evening meal.

Just then voices sounded outside—the door opened and a woman stepped lightly inside. Was it a phantom form such as Murray saw? Apparently not, for her garments were more sensible and better adapted to life in the woods. She did not appear surprised in the least to see us there. As she did not seem inclined to apologize for intruding, we concluded that it was our place to do so. But we were stopped by the remark that we did right, the door was never locked.

Soon Mr. Moore, the caretaker, came in; a general introduction followed and we were made welcome in true backwoods style "to such fare as they had," which, as it consisted of delicate steaming biscuits, the sweetest of butter, fragrant tea and other "fix-ins," as good enough for a king. It is altogether likely that if the king had been there the independent Californian would not have considered it worth his while to offer him anything better than he did us.

That night we listened to stories of hunting and

trapping, of mountain trails and forest paths, wonderful stories about the chasm of the Opalescent, the wildest gorge in the country. There for two miles the river foams and thunders over successive falls, one fully seventy feet in height, through rifts in the solid rocks five hundred feet in depth and scarcely eight feet across the top; of a line of traps sixteen miles long which the little woman who welcomed us should tend, making her rounds on snow-shoes, when the time for them came, ALONE. Think of that ye city weaklings as you take your airings on soft cushions, and then wonder if a life among the mountains is beneficial. When Mrs. Moore came to the woods she was brought in by her husband as an invalid. Now, with him she roams through the forest and mountains, goes hunting, fishing and guiding when there are ladies to accompany the parties.

"We came here to hunt and fish, wife and I, and

Indian Pass looking south from Summit Rock

the less people come the better it will please us," said John Moore, as we were leaving in the morning, "but if people will come, we will try and take care of them in the proper season. It is past that now, so you can put up your money, I don't want it." Then we left the couple who cared for no society save their own and the wild, free forests, with a friendly feeling in our hearts and the major part of two chickens in our knapsack—we needed them before we got through Indian Pass.

The old village is in the midst of wild and picturesque scenery. Just a little way north is Lake Henderson; from the head of which a trail leads to the Preston Ponds, the head of Cold River. Lake Harkness is one mile distant; Lake Andrews, specially noted for its quantities of trout, two. Toward the northeast to Calamity Pond it is four miles; to Lake Colden, six; Avalanche Lake, seven and a half; to the summit of Mt. Marcy, twelve miles.

The history of the place is brief and sad. In 1826, Messrs. Henderson, McMartin and McIntire had iron works at North Elba. One day an Indian showed them a piece of ore of remarkable purity, which he said came from a place where "water run over dam, we find plenty all same."

The services of the Indian were secured at once, at the rate of two shillings and what tobacco he could use per day, to conduct them to the place spoken of. Equipped for a long tramp they started, and on the second day arrived at the site of the present village, where they found, as the Indian had said, that the water literally poured over an iron dam. Hastening to Albany, a large tract of land embracing the principal ore beds in that vicinity was secured. Later forges were built and operations were commenced and a road cut from the Lower Works to Lake Champlain.

David Henderson, the moving spirit in the enterprise, was accidentally killed at a place now known as Calamity Pond. He always had a nervous terror of fire-arms, and on the day of his death his pistol was in the pack carried by his guide, who had laid it down to perform some service required of him. Thinking that it had fallen in a damp place, Mr. Henderson picked it up and dropped it on a rock nearby. With the motion came a sharp report from the pistol, the hammer of which had probably struck the rock in falling. Mr. Henderson fell to the ground saying, "I'm shot," and soon breathed his last! The hunter Cheney was there at the time, and tells a pitiful story of the grief of the little son, who was also with him. The body was borne out on the shoulders of workmen, and afterward a beautiful monument placed where he fell, bearing the inscription: "Erected by filial affection to the memory of our dear father, David Henderson, who accidentally lost his life on this spot by the premature discharge of a pistol, 3rd Sept., 1845."

Henderson monument at Calamity Pond

The whole enterprise had been financially a failure. In the death of Mr. Henderson the motive power was removed, and it was allowed to run down. Work gradually ceased, and three years after his death, the Upper Works were abandoned. The Lower Works were soon after left, and at last all that remained of the noisy village was an old Scotchman and family, who took care of the property and took in strangers that chanced to come that way, myself among the number.

Well do I remember the night when they sent us to sleep in one of the deserted houses having the reputation of being haunted. We did imagine that we heard curious sounds during the night, but whether uneasy spirits or some poor dog that we had robbed of his nest we could not tell. We quieted our fears and consciences, however, with the reflection that if it was a ghost, it would never think of looking for human beings in that bed, and if a dog, he certainly hadn't lost any thing worth mentioning in the operation. This is reminiscent, however, and occurred three years previous to the time when in 1873 the professor and myself tramped that way and beyond.

Chapter XIII

Avalanche Pass—Bill Nye and Hitch Up, Matilda!

Avalanche Lake is south of North Elba, where we spent the night after going through Indian Pass, high up among the mountains, 2,846 feet above tide, its waters like ice and its walls of black rock running down deep under and up almost perpendicularly hundreds of feet on either side. It is half a mile in length, and but a few rods in width. Between it and Lake Colden two immense slides descended the mountain long before the place was known, and are now covered with a heavy growth of timber, creating the little lake by imprisoning its waters in the narrow defile.

In 1867 another avalanche of loose rocks and earth swept downward from the summit and plunged into the sleeping lake below, nearly dividing it in two. This, the latest of any note, can be followed up to near the summit, but cannot be left without the aid of ladder or ropes. Where it started it is but eight or ten feet broad and as many deep, but increasing in volume as it descended, it tore its way through the soft rock until, at the bottom, the track is 75 feet wide and 40 or 50 deep.

William B. Nye, North Elba guide

Here in 1868 occurred a pleasant little episode in which "Bill Nye took a hand," which we wish to remark is not the Bill Nye who had that little affair with an "innocent" Oriental, but William B. Nye, a noted guide and hunter of North Elba. "Bill," as he is familiarly called, is one of those iron-moulded men just turned fifty, nearly six feet in height, powerfully built, knowing no danger or fatigue, and well versed in woodcraft. Silent, morose even if you in any way gain his dislike by a display of supposed superiority. By the way, he is but a type of the old time guides who, as a class, are modest, unassuming and withal, as noble a set of men as walk the earth. They have learned their own insignificance among the grand things of nature and silence in her solitude. They know what is becoming in man, and the upstart who presumes too much on his position as employer, expecting fawning servility, had better go back to civilization for all the extra comfort he can get out of a sojourn in the woods. If he likes you he cannot do too much for you, always ready and willing, and around the camp fire his tongue once loosed, the stories of wildwood life told in his quiet quaint style are full of interest—and a sure cure for the blues.

"Come, Bill—how about that adventure of yours at Avalanche Lake?" asked one of the party gathered around the blazing fire. We had all heard of it, but wanted the facts from the principal actor.

"What adventure?" asked Nye.

"Oh come, you know what one we mean; go ahead." So, after considerable innocent beating about the bush to ascertain the one meant, although it was perfectly evident that he knew all the time, Nye told his story:

"Well, boys—some of you may remember a party of three—a Mr. and Mrs. Fielding and their niece, from somewhere or other on the Hudson, that I went guiding in 1868. Mr. Fielding was rather a little man, one of those quick-motioned, impulsive sort who make up their minds quick and are liable to change it five minutes afterward, but a very generous gentleman withal. His wife was taller and heavier than he, would look things carefully over before she expressed an opinion, and when she made up her mind to do a thing she did it. The niece—Dolly they called her—was about seventeen years old, a splendid girl, handsome as a picture—and she knew it too—very sociable and willing to talk with any one; and I tell you boys, when I look at such a girl I sometimes feel as though maybe I made a mistake in living alone so long, but I'm too old a dog now to think of learning new tricks, so we will go on."

"Well! Our trip was to be from Nash's through Indian Pass to the Iron Works, then on to Mount

Marcy and back by way of Avalanche Pass. We got rather a late start from Nash's. All the boarders told Mrs. Fielding she could not go through to the Works that day, but she says, says she 'you'll see I shall—if the guide will show the way.' And she did go through, though we traveled the last three or four miles by torchlight. I tried to have her let me build a little camp and stay 'till daylight, but she said, 'No. You know what they said when we started. If you can find the way I am going through.' I told her I could find the way if it was darker than a stack of black cats and she says 'Lead on, I'll follow.' The last mile she carried her shoes in her hand, but she beat, and that was enough. The next day we went to Lake Colden and camped; the next to Mount Marcy and back to Colden Camp again.

"The following day we started to go through Avalanche Pass. You will remember the walls, hundreds of feet high on either side, that you can neither get over nor around without going around the mountain. Well, along one side is a shelf from two to four feet wide and about four feet under water that everybody don't know about. When we got there they wondered how we were to get past. I said I could carry them or I could build a raft, but to build a raft would take some time while I could carry them past in a few minutes. Provisions were getting short and the time set to be at North Elba, so Mr. Fielding says, 'Well, Matilda, what say you? Will you be carried over, or shall we make a raft?' Mrs. Fielding says: 'If Mr. Nye can do it, and thinks it safe, I will be carried over, to save time.' 'Well, Dolly, what do you say?' 'Oh, if Mr. Nye can carry Aunt over he can me, of course; I think it would be a novelty.' Mr. Fielding says: 'Well, we have concluded to be carried over, if you can do it safely.' I said, 'Perfectly safe. I have carried a man across that weighed 180

132

pounds, and a nervous old fellow at that.'

"I waded across and back to see if there had been any change in the bottom since I was there before. When in the deepest place the water is nearly up to my arms for a step or two but I had nothing with me then. When I got back Mrs. Fielding said she did not see how I was going to carry them across and keep them out of the water. I said, 'I will show you; who is going to ride first?' Mr. F. said, 'It is politeness to see the ladies safe first; so Matilda must make the first trip. She would let the politeness go, and would like to see Mr. F. go over first, but he said she had agreed to ride if I said it was safe; now he wanted to see her do it. 'So I will!' said she; 'How am I to do it?'

"I set down with my back against a rock that came nearly to the top of my shoulders, told her to step on the rock, put one foot over one side of my neck, the other over the other and sit down. That was what she did not feel inclined to do—she was going to climb on with both feet on one side, but her husband told her she must throw away her squeamishness and do as I told her, reminding her again of her word, which was enough. She finally sat down, very carefully but so far down my back that I could not carry her. I told her it wouldn't do. At last she got on and I waded in.

" 'Hurrah! there they go!' and 'Cling tight, Matilda!' shouted the young lady and the husband in the same breath. 'Hold your horse, aunt!' laughed Dolly. 'Your reputation as a rider is at stake; three cheers for Aunt Mazeppa!—I mean Aunt Matty—novel isn't it? Unique and pleasing. You'll beat Rarey, Auntie, that's what you'll do!'

"I had just got into the deep water and was steadying myself with one hand against the rocks and holding on to her feet with the other when, in spite of all I could do, she began to work down my back.

133

Hitch Up Matilda — (Stoddard drawing)

" 'Hitch up, Matilda! hitch up! why don't you hitch up?' screamed Mr. Fielding. I could hear him danc- ing around the rocks and stones on the shore, while I thought Dolly would have died laughing. And the more he yelled 'Hitch up,' the more she hitched down, and I began to think I would have to change ends, but by leaning way over forward, I managed to get her across safe and dry. Then 'How was she to get off?' I said, 'I will show you.' So I got down 'till her feet touched the ground and she walked off over my head, the two on the other side laughing and shouting all the time.

"Then came Dolly's turn. I told her that she must sit straight as a major general. She said she would— she'd let them see that all the money spent at riding schools hadn't been thrown away in her case. She wondered if any poet would immortalize her as they had Phil Sheridan. Then with some kind of a conundrum about Balaam (I never thought much of conundrums anyway) she got on and I took her over and unloaded her the same as I did her aunt. The rest was easy enough, rather more in my line too, and we got back all right. Of course I did no more than my duty at the time, but you can bet I kept pretty still about it for some time, until at last it leaked out. But there is one thing I would say, the ladies never made the slightest allusion to it in public, in my presence, at least, and for that—showing so much regard for the feelings of a bachelor—I shall be grateful to my dying day."

Chapter XIV

Keene Flats—Crawford's—Old Mountain Phelps

Keene Flats (now known as Keene Valley) undoubtedly possesses the loveliest combination of quiet valley and wild mountain scenery in the Adirondacks. Through it, from the south, come the sparkling waters of the East Branch of the Ausable, here flowing quietly along beneath overhanging maples and gracefully swaying elms, there rippling over glistening white sand. Now murmuring through pleasant meadow-land, anon dancing away among the stones. Then dashing down rocky race-ways to where, among the spray and foam of the cataract, it thunders and rumbles and roars as if angry with its prison walls. Then onward between the dark overhanging ledges outward through the northern portals and away to join its sister from the great Indian Pass above.

As soon as we approach from the north some of the beauties that have lent such a charm to this locality begin to appear in the restful groves of water maples, great massy drooping elms, clumps of alders fringing the river brink, great canopies of native grapevine clasping the rocks in loving embrace or festooned on the sturdy trees through which open up vistas of meadowland, a background of mountain green, and above all, summits of glittering granite.

On every side the mountains shut us in, rising right up out of the Flat instead of the gradual curve of a mountain from the plains, showing that the bottom of the valley is but the accumulated deposit of long ages, where the floods swept down from the mountains and left their sediment here in the notch between.

Through the gradually rising break in the mountains toward the west, Mount Marcy looks over into the valley, and there near its summit is the head of John's Brook, which joins the Ausable where we stand. On the east, among the group that surround the Giant another brook rises, and the water foaming down the sharp descent plunges over Phelps' Falls and joins the river a little below.

T. S. Perkins, it is said, was the first artist to find his way in, coming in 1857. When he went out it was with sketches of surprisingly lovely scenery found in a spot hitherto unknown among his fellows. The following year brought others, and soon, through their painting, the world learned of this quiet little nook and the appreciative lovers of nature found their way there. Among its first was R. M. Shurtleff, whose woods interiors with their filtered sunshine have placed him well up among artists.

We reached Keene from North Elba late in the afternoon, entered the gateway with the last rays of the sun crimsoning the eastern mountains, passed up along the valley in the golden twilight, and as night came down around us, drew up, at the hospitable door of the Crawfords. I say "draw up," for at Keene we fell in with a resident of the Flats, a genial, cheery old boy, whose nature is like his name, and whose age entitled him to hair of the same color. He invited us to ride and insisted on going considerably out of his way to be sure that we went right in ours. When we bade him good night, asking how we could repay him, he said, "Now don't you say nothing more about that; mebby you can do some one else the same good turn sometime." Then he drove away back through the darkness, as merry as a cricket, and we went inside.

Mr. Crawford was away on a hunting expedition; Mrs. Crawford was temporarily indisposed. The boys, though willing, were weak, the help had gone with the summer company! For a few minutes, the prospects of a hot supper looked dubious, but as every crisis brings forth some master of the situation, ours appeared in form of the accomplished wife of an eastern artist who did the honors of the establishment in a mountain costume, and with a completeness that could not have been improved. She joined heartily in the repast herself and leaving the mind of one of her guests at least, in a vague misty sort of wonder at the rather pleasant mixture of flaky biscuits, golden butter, rosebuds, fragrant tea, apple blossoms, pearls, oat meal, corn bread, sparkling eyes and cheeks the very picture of health. And *she* came to the woods an invalid. Is the free, pure air of the mountains and forests food? Try it and see.

Orson Schofield Phelps is what his parents named their baby, and "Old Mountain Phelps" is what everybody calls him now. His first name was given 57 years ago. He was born in the Green Mountain State, from which he came to the western part of Schroon when 14 years of age. He had an enthusiastic love for the woods, took to them on every possible occasion, and was a long time engaged in tracing out wild lot lines that extended far into the interior— "where in those times, deer and speckled trout were

"Old Mountain Phelps"

as plenty as mosquitoes on a damp day in July." He doesn't aspire to much as a hunter, but claims to have caught more trout than any other man in the country. In 1844 he was with Mr. Henderson at Adirondac.

Soon after, he married and settled in Keene Flats. In 1849 he made his first trip to the top of Marcy, crossing over Haystack around the head of Panther Gorge and to the summit, descending near where the main trail now runs, being the first man to get to the top from the east. He afterward cut what is now known as the Bartlett Mountain Trail, and soon guided two ladies up, which was considered quite a feat for them to perform and a feather in his cap. He also marked trails to the top of Hopkins' Peak, the Giant, up John's Brook to Marcy, and several others. He has made a valuable map of the mountain region around,

140

is a prized and regular contributor to a local paper, and has written a voluminous treatise on the Adirondack lakes and mountains, trees, birds, beasts, etc., which shows him to be a close observer and enthusiastic student of nature, and which will contain much valuable information when, as is promised, it is given to the public.

We found him at his home near the falls that bear his name; a little old man, about five foot six in height, muffled up in an immense crop of long hair and beard that seemed to boil up out of his collar band. Grizzly as the granite ledges he climbs, shaggy as the rough-barked cedar, but with a pleasant twinkle in his eye and an elasticity to his step equaled by few younger men. He likes to talk and delivers his sage conclusions and whimsical oddities in a cheery, chirripy, squeaky sort of tone—away up on the mountains as it were—an octave above the ordinary voice, somewhat suggestive of the warblings of an ancient chickadee.

Widow Beede's cottage at Keene Flats (Valley)

"So you wanted "Old Mountain Phelps" to show you the way, did you?" said he. "Well, I s'pose I kin do it. I'll be along as soon as the old woman'll bake me a shortcake. The wise man provides for a'nemergency, and hunger's one of 'em." So we returned to Crawford's for breakfast, after which, when the old man appeared with his little hatchet and big provision bag on his back. Mrs. Crawford had her nettlesome ponies brought around, and, with the artist's wife, carried up all to the Widow Beede's, where we bade them good-bye, delighted and duly grateful for the breezy ride of the morning.

Chapter XV

The Ausables—Camp Phelps—Tall Tales—
Homeward Bound

At the head of the Flats the Ausable from the south-west and Roaring Brook from the southeast join. When we reached the summit of the hill, south of the junction we saw a lovely view of the valley with the mountains on either side, stretching away for twenty miles toward the north.

"Roaring Brook comes mostly off of that," said Phelps, pointing to the east where the "Giant" lifted his scarred and rifted head high up in the air. "You see that chasm there? That is the lower end of Russell Falls. There is a gorge through that hill near 200 feet deep, the width of the river, and nearly perpendicular walls on either side, a continuous ragged fall all the way for half a mile, at no place more than 25 feet at one leap. When the water is low you can go through, but it isn't nice going at the best.

"See that bare rock near Smith Beede's? There is Roaring Brook Falls, the highest falls in the mountains; nearly 200 feet sheer at one leap, and I tell you it isn't much besides spray when it reaches the bottom. A mile above that—you see where Roaring Brook comes down the side of the "Giant" through that dark ravine—there is Chapel Pond. Up toward the top is another one, nearly as large, called 'Giant's Wash Bowl.' A narrow rim of rock holds it in on the lower side, and you can stand on its edge and throw a stone down into Chapel Pond, eight hundred feet below."

Resagonia or Sawtooth Mountain appears in the southwest, its curiously serrated crest gaining it the native title of Rooster's Comb. East of this is a round, rocky knob, known as Indian Head, and over this, a little further east, a sharp peak called Mount Colvin, after the superintendent of the Adirondack survey. Between the two mountains that drop downward at an acute angle, lies the lower Ausable Pond, four miles distant. Toward this notch we took our way down a little hill into the woods and up along brawling Gill Brook, over a path that is sometimes dignified by the name of wagonroad, but over which but few would attempt to ride.

"All things is possible and nothing impossible," said Phelps, diving into the bushes on one side of the road, and soon reappearing with a piece of band iron which he stowed away in his bag. "Like as not I will need this to mend an oar or something. Old Phelps is such an easy old critter to get along with that they take his boat, bang it 'round as much as they want to, maybe break an oar, and HE never'll make a fuss about it. Shouldn't wonder a bit if they had it off somewhere now."

After what seemed a long four-mile tramp through the woods, we came out in a little opening near the brow of a hill, and were just rising to look over when a fierce gust of wind from the other side set the old man's hat whirling back toward us. We succeeded in spearing it, then, as we turned and glanced out ahead, were surprised, almost dazzled by the wonderful beauty of the scene that flashed out so suddenly and unexpectedly on our astonished sight.

144

Lower Ausable Pond — (Stoddard drawing)

Ausable Pond in all its Swiss-like beauty was before us. We stood at the end of our road on the brow of a hill whose front had apparently been undermined, and ran sharply down to the water's edge, gleaming, drifting, unstable sand. On the left, close by was Indian Head, the side toward us all in sha-

dow; rough and jagged, standing like some grim sentinel to guard the narrow pass at his feet. Beyond was
Mount Colvin, the sides rising in places straight up
from the water, then backward to the sharp ridge
nearly 2,000 feet above, seemingly crowned with a
coronet of diamonds that flashed and glittered as the
water trickled down over the rocks and reflected
back the sun's bright beams. On the west was Resagonia, almost as abrupt, although trees grew from
its sides close down to the water's edge. Between
them the narrow Pond stretched away, its head hidden by the point on the right, its outlet at our feet.

Rainbow Falls is across the outlet to the northwest, back in the gorge. You can see where the brook
starts, away up on the Gothic Mountains, and trace
its course down the steep side until it is lost at the
base. We crossed the outlet and went up into the
cleft mountain-side, very like Ausable Chasm and
probably with a like origin. It extends only a short
distance but is very beautiful, the gray sides vertical
for something over a hundred feet, while huge rough
boulders lie at the bottom. Over the edge of the wall
at the north comes the stream, a skein of silk that
flutters along down the rocks until whipped and
ravelled, it reaches the bottom in spray, white as
clean wool. There, gathering its tiny drops together,
it goes softly singing down its emerald-paved steps
to the river below.

We descended to the outlet, where we compelled
Phelps' shortcake to assume an indisposed sort of
expression, then taking a boat started up the Pond,
over which the wind swept fiercely, picking up the
crests of the racing waves and dashing the spray in
our dripping faces, while the old man pulled and
talked, as though getting wet was the natural and
happy culmination of the very enjoyable trip.

The Lower Ausable Pond is about two miles in

length and only a few rods wide, in the very heart of the mountains. At the same time it is one of the lowest and easiest passes through them, providing always that a boat can be found in which to pass this point. The rocks on the east come down so straight into the water that it would be impossible to get past there. The west shore is almost as bad, although by some rough climbing among the huge masses that have fallen from the rocks, a person may succeed. Toward its head the water "shoaled," until it came above the surface in a strip of natural meadow, which gradually rising, was covered first with bushes then with a growth of heavy trees as though not the water alone but the soil that fills this trough of the mountains was passing slowly, like some great glacier, toward the plain. From the head a walk of a mile up along the brook brought us to the shores of the Upper Ausable, where Phelps expected to find his boat but did not.

"Just as I expected," said the old man finding matters as he had anticipated, "Old Phelps' boats belong to everybody but himself. Well, we haven't got much farther to go to my shanty. That's one satisfaction, and maybe they'll let us stay there all night, considering that it belongs to me." So we skirted the west shore a little way and came out at the shanty, where we found Crawford's party jubilant over the fourth deer they had taken in three days, and preparing supper to which we did full justice.

The Upper Ausable Pond is nearly two miles in length and perhaps a half mile wide. It is noted hunting ground as deer started in the mountains around, if not too far away, usually make for this water. There are two or three good log shanties on its shores, and a number of boats here and at the Lower Pond owned by the Keene Flats guides.

Camp Phelps, where we stopped that night, is one

of the most complete in its appointments and management of any shanty in the Adirondacks. The structure is of an elegant design, and built of magnificent logs cut and curved artistically with knots of various and unique patterns in bas relief. The main door is about 2½ by 5 feet, swings outward, and is locked with a string. It contains reception room, drawing room, private parlor and sleeping rooms en suite, with wardrobes sticking out all around the sides. The grand dining room is situated out on the lawn, which is quite extensive and furnished with hemlock extensions and stumps. This spacious structure is six by ten feet on the ground, between four and five feet high, and is surmounted by a Yankee roof of troughs in two layers, the upper layer inverted, covering the crevices in the lower so as to exclude the rain. But separated far enough to give perfect ventilation. This chef d'oeuvre of architecture is luxuriously upholstered throughout with spruce boughs. In the culinary department is a stupendous range which floods the drawing room with light. In short, it contains all the modern improvements, including hot and cold water, which is carried to every part of the establishment in pails.

Stories at Camp Phelps — (drawing by Stoddard)

Here we gathered—Crawford's party of seven, and ours, ten in all, besides two or three dogs, in a space about six by eight feet square. While the fire snapped and flickered filling the shanty with dancing shadows, stories of hunting and fishing adventures were told that all were expected to believe because they were personal experiences, although occasionally one would have a familiar sort of sound with the exception of names and dates. Stories of personal prowess were common and culminated in one of a man who could pick up a two barrel iron kettle by the edge with his teeth, and the assertion by another that he knew a man who could perform the same feat sitting in the kettle himself when he lifted it.

These, however, were making light of serious subjects, so Phelps told his bear story of how one day near the Boreas, he saw a big bear coming on the run after him and he, armed with only a little ax. But when the bear got within twenty feet of him he yelled, "Halt," which stopped the bear . . . he couldn't prevaricate, he did it with his little hatchet. He didn't feel scared any, only stirred up like, but the bear reversed ends and made off as fast as it could wabble.

Then Uncle Harvey told all about how he killed a bear with a pitchfork once, and a moose with a club, after tiring him out in the deep snow. "But, by gawl, boys," said he, "When Dick Estes tumbled over backwards on his snow shoes and the critter gave a lunge for him, I thought it was all up with him, but I just gave command to the boys, and at him we went, and, by gawl, the way we laid it on his old hide was a caution. And there lay Dick, square on his back, looking up, thinkin' that every minute was his last, and, by gawl, I just managed to get a lick at the critter that fetched him just as he was standin' over Dick so." And the old hunter assumed a position indicative of an enraged moose preparing to come down on an unfortunate chap on his back in the snow, who couldn't turn over on account of his snow-shoes.

Thus each had his story to tell until time to turn in, when four of the party went across the pond to another camp, leaving six of us to occupy a space six feet long by six feet wide. There we slept on edge, like a box of well-packed sardines, until daylight. Then each man got up and cut a chunk of venison, salt pork or bacon as taste dictated, and each man for himself waltzed around that stove in the six by ten shanty until he had warmed it through enough to suit. Or, disguising pieces of raw material in an outside coating of bread, he proceeded to stow it away with that appearance of keen enjoyment displayed by the average boy in taking a pill. Then some rushed away to put out the dogs and others to the various runways to watch.

The old man now gave his attention to some sort of a stew, which, as he had made no calculations on staying out all night, and the camp supplies had run low in the particular materials needed, was partially a failure. The Professor, (Charles Oblenis, Stoddard's brother-in-law) with a homesick sort of expression on his face, was picking away at an ancient piece of bacon. Another enthusiastic individual who had wallowed in an ecstasy of bliss, theoretically over venison steak, broiled at the blazing camp fire, was engaged in preparing a savory strip of the same, which as he forgot to apply salt, and got hold of a piece, but just moderately warm. At the first bite, it roused a rebellious feeling within him, bringing with full force those saddest of all words, "it might have been (done)," but was not ordained.

Then at last, as his mind kept running on accounts of shipwrecked people who had to eat each other or starve, and cannibalism seemed imminent, one of the guides came in like a dove bringing—not the olive branch exactly—but a bag of oatmeal, which he made into pancakes! And those pancakes went to our hearts and stomachs like the blissful ecstasy of love's young dream. We were saved! And while we ate he baked and brought them forward; none of your little patty cakes, but great big ones the size of the frying pan, and as light as sea foam almost, making, with maple sugar, a breakfast, the which when suggested, makes my mouth water to this day. And the more we ate the happier he seemed to feel. And those cakes touched a chord in the breast of one individual at least that will vibrate for all time, and if ever permitted to go there again he would not ask for a more willing assistant or, if reports be true, a better guide than Theo. White of Keene Flats, the author of those glorious pancakes.

After breakfast Phelps took us up the inlet, with its dark borders of balsams and tamarack, to the Marcy trail. There we bid him a regretful adieu, for we had become attached to the cheery old man

Root's Hotel, Schroon River

of the mountains in our short acquaintance. We started on our tramp of sixteen miles, out through the woods to Root's, feeling that we were nearing friends who would be glad to welcome us home; clearer in thought and stronger in body than when we entered. Glad to go back but sad at the thought of leaving the mountains, over which we saw the storm-clouds gather, break and roll away, leaving them, kissed by the loving sunshine, clean, grand, strong and eternal as the hand that made them.

The End

ABOUT THE EDITOR

Born in Canton, N.Y., De Sormo grew up in Malone. Educated at Franklin Academy, Hamilton College and New York University (M.A.) he did further graduate work at Teachers College, Columbia University. Taught English, Speech and Drama at Indian River School, New Smyrna, Florida; Malverne and Irvington-on-Hudson High Schools.

Recently retired from public school teaching, he is currently lecturer in Adirondack history at North Country Community College in Saranac Lake.

Owns extensive S. R. Stoddard and Adirondackana collections. Author of *Told Around the Campfire,* (the Van Hoevenberg story) *Noah John Rondeau, Adirondack Hermit* and 30 articles on the northern region of New York State. These have appeared in *The Adirondac, Adirondack Life, North Country Life, York State Tradition, Franklin Historical Review, New York Folklore Quarterly,* and *Down East* magazines.

Historian, Town of Harrietstown; partner in North Country Books; president of the Lake Placid-North Elba Historical Society, Trustee of the Franklin County Historical Society, he is also a member of the Wilderness Society, the Adirondack Park Association (of which he is chairman of Promotion and Advertising Committee), the Adirondack Mountain Club and the Adirondack Forty-sixers.